The Passionate Church

Also by Mike Slaughter

Change the World

Christmas Is Not Your Birthday

Dare to Dream

Hijacked

Momentum for Life

Money Matters

Real Followers

Renegade Gospel

shiny gods

Spiritual Entrepreneurs

The Christian Wallet

UnLearning Church

Upside Living in a Downside Economy

For more information, visit www.MikeSlaughter.com

MIKE SLAUGHTER

with Karen Perry Smith

THE PASSIONATE CHURCH

Ignite Your Church and Change the World

Church Stories by Amy Forbus • Facilitator's Guide by Jacob Armstrong

Abingdon Press / Nashville

THE PASSIONATE CHURCH:
IGNITE YOUR CHURCH AND CHANGE THE WORLD

This book is printed on elemental chlorine-free paper.

Library of Congress Cataloging-in-Publication data applied for.
978-1-5018-1503-4

16 17 18 19 20 21 22 23 24 25 — 10 9 8 7 6 5 4 3 2 1
MANUFACTURED IN THE UNITED STATES OF AMERICA

*To the hundreds of faithful servants
of Ginghamsburg Church,
who give sacrificially of their time,
talents, and treasure toward Christ's mission*

Contents

Welcome to *The Passionate Church* 9

1. Developing Principled Christian Leaders 19

2. Engaging in Ministry with the Poor 47

3. Creating New and Renewed Congregations 73

4. Improving Global Health 103

Epilogue 131

Notes 133

Facilitator's Guide 141

Welcome to
The Passionate Church

*I am not afraid that the people called Methodist should
ever cease to exist either in Europe or America. But I am
afraid lest they should only exist as a dead sect, having the
form of religion without the power. And this undoubtedly
will be the case unless they hold fast both the doctrine,
spirit and discipline from which they first set out.*[1]
—John Wesley, Founder of the Methodist Movement

IT'S FRIDAY

My friend Tony Campolo, a well-known speaker, preacher,
author, and activist, is a spellbinding storyteller. I have

heard Tony speak on several occasions, including a few times at Ginghamsburg United Methodist Church in Tipp City, Ohio, where I have served as lead pastor for almost four decades. Tony's delivery is always powerful. But I would have to say that my all-time favorite anecdote of Tony's is the story of a "preach-off" held at Tony's largely African American church in West Philadelphia several years ago. Tony was one of the pastors preaching and ended his turn in the pulpit feeling pretty good about himself and the effectiveness of his oratory. As Tony tells it though, he was soon humbled when his seasoned, elderly black pastor took the platform and out-preached Tony, summing up his message with five words, repeated in a captivating cadence that soon brought the congregation to its feet: "It's Friday, but Sunday's coming!"[2]

In the mainline American church right now, it feels like Friday. Recent blogs have declared the death of Christianity in America and speculated that Jesus has left his church. If all a non-Christian knew about Christ's church was what he or she had read or heard in the media, that person would no doubt agree. Based on the headlines and pundits, the church appears stodgily institutionalized and shrinking—irrelevant at best and vehemently exclusive and fearmongering at its worst. Headlines about the president of a Christian university encouraging his students to arm themselves certainly helped to muddy the already murky waters. Daily we seem to hear more about what the church is against rather than what we are to stand for: being the hands, feet, and voice of Jesus to the world that "God so loved."

Sadly, the available data only furthers our impending sense of gloom and doom. In 2010, the United Methodist Call to Action Steering Team commissioned Towers Watson, a global professional services firm, to measure the vitality of United Methodist congregations in the United States. The project reviewed 32,228 such congregations in the United States during a three- to five-year period, finding that 36 percent of United Methodist churches are either dying or already are dead and simply haven't realized it yet.[3]

That is not the only discouraging news for The United Methodist Church. Active elders (ordained, credentialed clergy) are aging. The Lewis Center for Church Leadership reports that as of 2015, 55 percent of all active elders were between the ages of fifty-five and seventy-two, the highest historical percentage for that age group.

Even a recent report from the Pew Center added to the bad news bandwagon. According to Pew, America's religiously unaffiliated increased from 16 percent to 23 percent from 2007 to 2014. Weekly church attendance dropped from 40 percent to 36 percent, and fewer Americans prayed daily.[4] So, it sure does feel like Friday. Is Sunday coming? Yes—God's church will not fail, because its Founder won't fail. This is why I was compelled to write *The Passionate Church: Ignite Your Church and Change the World.*

WHAT TO EXPECT IN
THE PASSIONATE CHURCH

The genesis for *The Passionate Church* can be traced back to 2008 when The United Methodist Church, concerned about these and other alarming trends, moved to take action. That year the church's General Conference designated Four Areas of Focus for all levels of the church, designed to provide a way forward and revitalize the movement.

1. Developing Principled Christian Leaders
2. Engaging in Ministry with the Poor
3. Creating New and Renewed Congregations
4. Improving Global Health

When the Four Areas of Focus were announced, I first evaluated them against what I saw as the most vital dimensions embodied within Jesus' practices of ministry. They resonated. I then began to assess Ginghamsburg Church's ministry and mission in light of these four areas. In fact, for all Jesus' followers, I believe those four areas are at the core of what it means to be a passionate church, a church committed to world change and life transformation.

In *The Passionate Church*, we will explore in detail each of these Four Areas of Focus from three vantage points. For each area we will first look to God's Word to assess scriptural support and context. Does the pursuit of an area truly reflect Kingdom priorities of Jesus, or is it simply a human construct with little likelihood of impact or Kingdom success?

We will then reach back into Methodist history to explore the founding principles and practices of our eighteenth-century Wesleyan beliefs. Is the area of focus timeless—proven yesterday, pertinent today, doable tomorrow—and in line with our theology?

Finally we will explore what each area of focus can look like when put into action. We will share stories about faith communities of all sizes and geographies that have turned Passionate Church principles into purposeful action, and we will suggest a few ideas that might be helpful to other churches in moving forward.

The Facilitator's Guide at the end of the book is designed for pastors and church leaders who want to study the book together, take action, and hold each other accountable, whether inside a single congregation or across congregations.

Before we dive in, let's briefly preview these four essential areas along with inspiring stories you'll read about some churches across the United States and the world that are doing great work in these areas.

THE FOUR AREAS OF FOCUS

1. Developing Principled Christian Leaders

Principled Christian leaders are Kingdom difference makers. These folks are more than just fans of Jesus; they have made the commitment to follow Jesus in the costly way of the cross. They have moved beyond volunteerism to a lifestyle of servanthood.

Disciples of Jesus make whole-life commitments to be the hands, feet, and bank accounts of Jesus in the world. By following Jesus in the way of the cross, a disciple adopts a lifestyle of nonconformity with the values of the world. John Wesley was only twenty-two and a Fellow at Lincoln College in Oxford University when he become aware of a gnawing need in his life: "I was convinced more than ever of the impossibility of being half a Christian, and determined to be all devoted to God—to give Him all my soul, my body, and my substance"[5]

Like Wesley, a congregation will never experience effective mission if a strategy for "all devoted" discipleship is not the first priority.

Stories:

- A Culture of Call: "Part of the Atmosphere"
- Creating a Path for Young People to Explore Christian Leadership
- Christmas Institute (Philippines)

2. Engaging in Ministry with the Poor

When Jesus announced the beginning of his messianic mission in his hometown synagogue, he read from chapter 61 of Isaiah. The Gospel of Luke describes the passage this way:

13

"The Spirit of the Lord is on me,
    because he has anointed me
    to proclaim good news to the poor.
He has sent me to proclaim freedom for the prisoners
    and recovery of sight for the blind,
to set the oppressed free,
        to proclaim the year of the Lord's favor."

(Luke 4:18-19)

The mission statement of Jesus—and therefore of Christians—is clear. Our ministry must be intentionally engaged with the needs of the poor, the prisoner, the blind, and the oppressed. If our energies and resources do not result in good news for the poor, then you can bet your last dollar we are not about the gospel of Jesus Christ!

The passage in Isaiah that Jesus read goes on to describe the commitment that the members of the messianic mission will be engaged in: "They will rebuild the ancient ruins and restore the places long devastated; they will renew the ruined cities that have / been devastated for generations" (Isaiah 61:4).

John Wesley understood that ministry with the poor was essential to the practice of Christian faith. Perhaps Robert Solomon put Wesley's words best when he wrote, "Our ministry to the poor becomes a means of grace by which God does His work of holiness in us. It becomes a way by which God perfects us in His love and makes us Christ-like."[6] The early Methodists demonstrated this commitment to the poor through the development of schools, clinics, prison ministries, clothing and feeding programs, and various other ministries.

Stories:

- From "Ministry to" to "Ministry With"
- Grace-Driven Outreach Creates Diverse Community
- Give the Helping Hand (Russia)

3. Creating New and Renewed Congregations

The church growth movement, popular among many congregations in the late twentieth century, tended to focus on expansion within a single church, breaking through barriers of two hundred, four hundred, eight hundred members and beyond. The New Testament church, on the other hand, was a church-multiplying ministry.[7] The rapid spread of the early Christian movement took place through the multiplication of relatively small congregations. Even though the number of converts grew to thousands in many cities, the New Testament often refers to "the church that meets at their house" (1 Corinthians 16:19, Romans 16:5). My friend and mentor Howard Snyder makes the prophetic point:

> Growth comes by the multiplication of congregations, not necessarily by the multiplication of church buildings or institutional structures. If the church can grow only as fast as buildings are built or pastors are academically trained or budgets are expanded, then growth is limited to the resources available for these purposes. The early church was strikingly unlimited by such factors. And these are not the real hindrances to church growth today.[8]

Experience reveals that the most successful new church starts or restarts come from healthy local churches. Healthy living organisms reproduce. The church, ever striving to reach and serve more people, must meet people where they are and tailor each new community to the people it seeks to serve.

Stories:

- A Gateway of Hope
- Making a Place Inviting to New People
- Participate in Our Dream (Malawi)

4. Improving Global Health

Jesus has given us as his disciples the mandate to heal the sick (see Mark 6:7-13; Luke 9:1). Early Methodists understood the call to influence health care in the eighteenth century as a necessity in the mandate of proclaiming the whole of the gospel, and today the church has become a key player in fighting diseases such as malaria and AIDS and promoting initiatives that improve well-being throughout the world.

Global health also includes our own well-being, as expressed in John Wesley's writings about healthy nutrition and the value of exercise:

> We may strengthen any weak part of the body by constant exercise. Thus, the lungs may be strengthened by loud speaking, or walking up an easy ascent; the digestion and nerves by riding; the arms and hams by strong rubbing them daily.[9]

We minister in a time when more than one-third (35.7 percent) of adults in the United States are considered obese. More than one in twenty (6.3 percent) have extreme obesity. Almost three in four men (74 percent) are considered to be overweight or obese. Obesity has led to type 2 diabetes being increasingly prevalent among both adults and children.[10]

Whether in the local community or around the world, a growing number of churches are reaching out through ministries that fight disease and promote healthy lifestyles.

Stories:

- Connecting With Global Health Movement Revitalizes Small Church
- Improving Global Health, One Shipping Container at a Time
- Texting to Save Lives (Congo)

SUNDAY'S COMING!

Although it's been feeling like Friday, why am I convinced Sunday's coming? During the church's more than two thousand years of existence, troubled times have been followed by cycles of renewal. My United Methodism "tribe" was birthed out of a movement started by John Wesley in the mid-eighteenth century because Wesley believed that the institutional church of his day had become ineffective and misguided.[11] Wesley reconnected Christ followers with the power of the Holy Spirit and birthed a new, transformative movement that actively served the mission of Jesus in the world. In our own time, students in the Jesus Movement and the Campus Crusade for Christ served as agents of renewal and reconciliation, actively serving on behalf of social justice issues such as racism and sexism.

The church is not dead. But it is definitely time for resurrection; it's time for Sunday. Churches must remember who we are and whose we are, and rise up off of our blessed assurances to take positive, powerful, and Christ-filled action in these Four Areas of Focus. In the words of movement maker John Wesley, our churches—and we Jesus followers—must begin again to "hold fast both the doctrine, spirit and discipline from which they first set out."

Let's get started.

1
Developing Principled Christian Leaders

My gracious Master and my God, assist me to proclaim,
to spread through all the earth abroad the honors of thy
name.
—Charles Wesley, "O For a Thousand Tongues to Sing"

AT THE CORE

During his three-year ministry, Jesus frequently attracted crowds for healing and teaching, but after his crucifixion most members of the five thousand families served during the miracle of the fishes and loaves were nowhere in sight. Jesus knew that the secret of creating a vibrant movement was not in drawing crowds but in selecting and growing a core group of disciples to serve as the movement's leaders. Luke 6 portrays how Jesus first identified the twelve apostles, eleven of whom would birth the early church. In Luke 10, Jesus sent out seventy-two disciples to proclaim that the kingdom of God had come near. Then in Acts 1 and 2, Luke reported that 120 believers gathered together after Jesus' resurrection and ascension to pray and await the gifting of the Holy Spirit.

These are not particularly impressive "attendance" numbers by today's church standards, but the true power of Christianity is at the core, not on the outskirts of a crowd. As Jesus reminded us in his prayer to the Father for the disciples in John 17:17-19, the leader's holiness—or sanctification—is critical: "Sanctify them by the truth; your word is truth. As you sent me into the world, I have sent them into the world. For them I sanctify myself, that they too may be truly sanctified."

Easy "believism" without sacrifice is not a viable shortcut, as Dietrich Bonhoeffer compellingly wrote in his classic book *The Cost of Discipleship*. John Wesley also understood that any thriving movement begins with impassioned and sanctified leaders who have caught a vision that transforms into a whole-life focus. Wesley's "methods" of holiness became foundational to the roots of the Wesleyan movement and the birth of Methodism.

TURNING THE CONVENTIONAL MODEL UPSIDE DOWN

My journey at Ginghamsburg Church started thirty-seven years ago when I crossed its doorstep for the first time at age twenty-seven. Ginghamsburg was classified then as a rural church, located three miles south of the village of Tipp City, Ohio, and sixteen miles north of Dayton, a small city with an approximate population of 140,000.[1]

When I received the call from my United Methodist district superintendent letting me know that the bishop planned to appoint me to Ginghamsburg, I was serving as a youth pastor in a moderately affluent "country club" church in Cincinnati. The church had a good-sized budget, and I as its youth pastor had even bigger dreams. God had been working in and through the youth ministry that I led to grow a deeply discipled group of students who were ready to change the world for Jesus. Needless to say, I was ill prepared for an appointment to a small, rural, family-controlled church that was perfectly content to remain just that. I realized from the beginning that the biggest key to change would be transforming the congregation's mind-set from a consumer mentality to one that was missional.

Many of our United Methodist churches resemble what I call the conventional church model, as depicted by the triangle below. Ginghamsburg in 1979 certainly did.

In this conventional church model, the real power and authority are typically held by the middle layer—the committees. At Ginghamsburg, a church of ninety attendees when I arrived that shrank to fewer than sixty in my first six months, about twenty people staffed those committees, with the primary function of controlling and approving the ministry that I as the pastor was then supposed to go out and do. Clearly, one man or woman being the hands and feet of Jesus under the strict jurisdiction of a committee is not going to be effective. The pastor eventually becomes the cork in the bottle, limiting ministry and mission to the narrowest of confines. Given how pervasive the conventional church model is, it's no wonder we hear so much about pastor burnout. Over time, the pastor basically becomes the caregiver to a stagnant and declining congregation, and the mission of discipleship is never fulfilled. In a few years, the pastor moves on to another conventional church, and both the previous church and the new church continue in the downward spiral of stagnation that eventually leads to death.

My job at Ginghamsburg was to help the church transform itself from the conventional church model to one that more closely resembles the triangle depicted below, which I call the unlimited-exponential model.

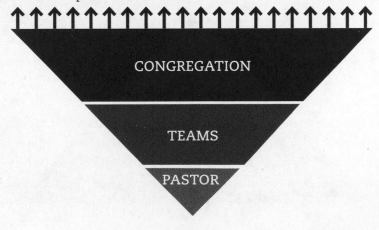

When the church structure matches this model, the pastor is not the doer of the ministry. He or she becomes the vision crier, the equipper, and the behind-kicker, working to build and equip the teams who will then work through the entire congregation to deploy ministry and mission throughout the community and world.

As Ginghamsburg eventually moved into and embraced the unlimited-exponential church model, the servants of Ginghamsburg Church were empowered to impact hundreds of thousands of lives through a wide variety of ministries and mission initiatives that were dreamed, staffed, and deployed by the priesthood of all believers—not just the pastor.

EMPOWERING LEADERS WHO EMPOWER OTHERS

I did not invent the unlimited-exponential model of what church can be. One of the first leadership gurus who named the need to empower lay leaders for the mission can be found in Scripture: Moses' father-in-law, Jethro. In Exodus 18, the Israelites under Moses' leadership and God's provision had escaped their Egyptian captors after four hundred years of enslavement. The Israelites were camped in the desert when Moses received a message alerting him that Jethro was coming to visit. When Jethro arrived, he became deeply engaged as he listened to Moses share all that God had done to free his people.

The next day, though, Jethro spotted a major stumbling block in Moses' management style. Moses would sit from sunup to sundown each day serving as the people's chaplain, commander-in-chief, and arbiter, hearing arguments, settling suits, keeping the peace, and shepherding the flock. This role may sound familiar

A Culture of Call:
"Part of the Atmosphere"

St. John's United Methodist Church of Aiken, South Carolina, sees about 850 people in worship each Sunday. It offers Disciple Bible Study, various small and large group studies, English as a Second Language classes, and is beginning a ministry with the Hispanic community led by the new bilingual associate pastor.

"This is a church that has a high level of commitment to discipleship," says senior pastor the Reverend Dr. Tim McClendon, who admits he has trouble keeping up with all that St. John's offers to enrich the Christian journey.

What he does keep up with is the fruit of such commitment: God's calling on individual lives. Eight ordained clergy have emerged from the congregation in recent years, and several current seminary students discerned their calls to ministry while at St. John's.

"It's more subliminal than intentional," McClendon says about the culture of call within St. John's. "It's part of the atmosphere."

Those with an aptitude for ministry often spend a summer during college as an intern on the St. John's staff, in youth or children's ministries, shadowing a pastor, or assisting with hospital visitation. The church puts financial encouragement behind that atmosphere too; about fifteen years ago, it began a seminary scholarship fund. The fund currently makes it possible for one of the church's members to attend Duke Divinity School.

McClendon and others on staff take notice of those they think may have a calling beyond being a Christian layperson. "I try to very carefully and appropriately, at the right time, say, 'Hey, the Lord's going to use you in very special ways, whether you're a layperson or a minister,'" he said.

For example, one young teen in the church "seems to exhibit God in his heart and in his life, and he's very sincere. . . . This kid might just have it," he said. "And so, I've talked to him and I've mentioned it to his parents, and they agree."

The South Carolina Conference Board of Ordained Ministry, on which McClendon sits, makes a point of connecting with young people at Revolution, that conference's annual youth retreat. "A part of the Revolution youth event is a special invitation to those who might feel called to Christian service," McClendon says. "We have an orientation time with them after the concert—a specific part of the weekend where we basically put out this call to ministry."

And it's not just young people being called—others a bit older are pursuing their call to ministry as a second career.

"It may be that underscoring the ministry of the priesthood of *all* believers to the point that everybody's so involved means that for some, it's not a far reach to step from being a dedicated Christian layperson to being a clergyperson," he said. "Because they see it as sort of a natural part of life, it doesn't freak them out, the notion of 'God might be calling me to do more.'"

to many pastors, who find themselves scurrying from committee gathering to board meeting, from hospital bed to nursing home, while also trying to write an engaging weekly sermon—a perfect recipe for burning out or even dropping out. Jethro recognized immediately that this style did not represent the best use of Moses' leadership gifts and calling. He told Moses: "What you are doing is not good. You and these people who come to you will only wear yourselves out. The work is too heavy for you; you cannot handle it alone" (Exodus 18:17-18).

Jethro reminded Moses that his best leadership gifts were prophetic teaching and visionary leadership, not being an arbitration specialist. As a result, Jethro advised Moses to become a leader of leaders, identifying and mentoring a cadre of godly folks who would listen to and judge the peoples' disputes. Jethro also wisely noted that some of these new leaders would be more capable than others:

> "But select capable men from all the people—men who fear God, trustworthy men who hate dishonest gain—and appoint them as officials over thousands, hundreds, fifties and tens. Have them serve as judges for the people at all times, but have them bring every difficult case to you; the simple cases they can decide themselves." (Exodus 18:21-22)

Moses had the good sense to act on sound advice.

> He chose capable men from all Israel and made them leaders of the people, officials over thousands, hundreds, fifties and tens. They served as judges for the people at all times. The difficult cases they brought to Moses, but the simple ones they decided themselves. (Exodus 18:25-26)

When the pastor is the lone doer of the mission at the top of a lonely pyramid, the mission is limited and soon stifled. When the pastor becomes the equipper and deployer of the saints, mission multiplication is limitless.

The ultimate New Testament example of this leadership empowerment principle in action is Jesus himself. After deep prayer and discernment, Jesus chose and then poured himself into twelve disciples, eleven of whom would be the founding leaders of a movement that changed the world forever. What I have always found fascinating about Jesus' selection of leaders was their diversity. Look at the list in Matthew 10:2-4:

> These are the names of the twelve apostles: first, Simon (who is called Peter) and his brother Andrew; James son of Zebedee, and his brother John; Philip and Bartholomew; Thomas and Matthew the tax collector; James son of Alphaeus, and Thaddaeus; Simon the Zealot and Judas Iscariot, who betrayed him.

The group included fishermen, a tax collector, and even a zealot (part of a first-century political movement that sought to overthrow Roman rule). At first blush, these men would appear to have nothing in common. In fact, Matthew and Simon were in essence enemies, the former an agent of Rome's power and influence and the latter an advocate for Rome's overthrow. This inclusive selection and deployment of unlikely people created a movement that not only reset the calendar for all future days to come but is transforming the world to the present day. Note that not a single disciple was part of the ordained clergy class of the day.

When it comes to Kingdom work, there is room at the table for everyone. Jesus may have deployed diversity toward the greatest accomplishment of the ages—the establishment of his church— but he was not the first in Scripture to see the value of casting a wide net across the potential talent pool. Nehemiah 3 is one of those chapters in the Old Testament that we love to skip, since it has little exciting action and is filled with names that are hard to pronounce. Yet the people behind those names were chosen by Nehemiah to rebuild the wall around Jerusalem in only fifty-two days, an astounding accomplishment in an era before cranes, bulldozers, and power tools. The variety of wall laborers ranged from Eliashib the high priest to Levites, goldsmiths, perfume-makers, the sons of rulers, and the daughters of Shallum. No one was excluded from the opportunity to serve or lead.

Diversity is essential; however, it only takes us so far. Not everyone is called and equipped for leadership.

Deploying diversity in all its forms toward the mission is only one component for growing lay leadership within the church. The Bible has a great deal to say about the qualifications for leadership, and it deserves our consideration. Popular wisdom tells us that desperate times call for desperate measures, but we can never become so desperate that we risk the core leadership value of integrity. Our leaders, whether clergy or lay, must walk the walk and talk the talk.

MIND THE GAP

Not long ago, I was part of a team of United Methodist clergy that spent time in England, revisiting the roots of our Wesleyan movement. Stops included many important landmarks from the ministry of John Wesley in York, Epworth, Oxford, Bristol, and London. In London we frequently took the subway, also known as the Tube, to move about the city. At each stop, a voice came over the public address system cautioning those exiting to "mind the gap"—in other words, to watch our step as we navigated the space between the edge of the train car and the start of the platform. If we weren't careful, the result could be painful, or even dangerous. The more I heard "mind the gap," the more the Spirit impressed it upon me as an appropriate aphorism for leading with integrity.

Too often, what we as Jesus followers, much less church leaders, claim as central beliefs do not match our core actions. There is a gap between what we proclaim and what we do. For instance, I suspect most of our United Methodist clergy believe it is important to take care of our bodies, the temple of the living God. Yet a 2015 report on United Methodist clergy health showed that 42 percent of the survey respondents were obese and an additional 37 percent qualified as overweight. The report indicated that this clergy obesity percentage was much higher than a demographically matched sample of US adults at large. Our actions as clergy, in other words, do not match our claimed beliefs in this area.[2] Ultimately what we do or don't do is the real indicator of what we value. Watch what I do, for what I do is what I really believe.

Many of our church folks would claim a belief that being in regular corporate worship is important. Yet many church Baby Boomers have transitioned into what I call the "up and down" generation. Each Sunday they are either up in the mountains or down at the lake, spending time with grandkids and enjoying their relative affluence. I can relate—I love the mountains *and* my grandkids. But many of us who used to be in worship weekly now consider ourselves "regulars" if we show up once a month, or even once a quarter.

Once again there is a gap, as what we espouse and what we do fall out of alignment. Authentic, principled leaders within the church do not have that luxury. We must be ever mindful of the gap. That is one reason I pray each day, "Lord, today let me be who you need me to be and who my family believes me to be." As Jesus cautioned us in Matthew 7:21, "Not everyone who says to me, 'Lord, Lord,' will enter the kingdom of heaven, but only the one who does the will of my Father who is in heaven."

One of my favorite descriptions of a biblical leader is Psalm 78:72: "And David shepherded them with integrity of heart; with skillful hands he led them." Principled leadership requires both skill of hands and integrity of heart. We cannot abdicate either of those leadership criteria on behalf of the other. And yet in our humanness it is so easy to do so. Natural talent is easier to spot; discerning the integrity that must underlie it can take more time.

Even the prophet Samuel struggled to discern integrity in his initial anointing of David as the future king of Israel. As described in 1 Samuel 16, per God's instructions Samuel traveled to Bethlehem to anoint God's new choice of king after King Saul's character proved fatally flawed. When David's oldest brother Eliab appeared, Samuel was convinced that the tall, healthy, mature-looking young man had to be God's choice. God corrected Samuel, saying, "Do not consider his appearance or his height, for I have rejected him. The Lord does not look at the things people look at. People look at the outward appearance, but the Lord looks at the heart" (v. 7).

Paul also was mindful of what it means to be a "principled" leader. In 1 Timothy 3:1-13, Paul advised his protégé Timothy about selecting leaders within the church:

- Those aspiring to leadership are to desire "a noble task," not self-promotion or self-aggrandizement (v. 1).
- A leader's public life must be above reproach; he or she must be temperate, self-controlled, and hospitable, and should not be a violent person, an overindulger in alcohol, nor a lover of money (vv. 2-3).

- The leader's private life must be in alignment with this public image. Leaders are faithful to their spouses, strong disciplers of their children, and successful managers on the home front (vv. 4-5, 12).
- Leaders must be well grounded in the faith, not recent converts; the stakes are too great. As Paul described, "They must keep hold of the deep truths of the faith with a clear conscience" and "first be tested" (vv. 6, 9-10).
- Leaders also need to have, or be coachable in, the necessary skills required for a given leadership position. Paul describes this for Timothy's list as "able to teach" (v. 2). In other words, as the psalmist noted, "skill of hands" is essential along with "integrity of heart."

Too often we are tempted to grab the first "Eliab" who comes along and appears to look the part. If you searched your pews in your mind's eye as you read Paul's list and came up wanting, your church may have another serious gap—a discipleship "gap" that we had better be "minding." The Towers Watson findings reinforce the criticality of strong disciples for successful leadership.

One of the key factors the report identifies as driving laity effectiveness in churches is the lay leaders' demonstration of a vital personal faith, including disciplines of prayer and Bible study, regular worship attendance, proportional giving, mission participation, and personal faith-sharing.[3] These disciples rotated through multiple positions, using a variety of gifts in various servant leadership roles over time.

Further, the study linked lay leadership with pastor leadership: an important attribute of pastor leadership was shown to be the developing, coaching, and mentoring of lay leaders. Clearly, equipping the saints by empowering the priesthood of all believers is essential for accomplishing the mission of Jesus.

Creating a Path for Young People to Explore Christian Leadership

An idea from a South Georgia campus minister and the backing of a young clergy task force has produced an immersive experience for young people considering a calling to ordained ministry.

Rev. C. J. Harp envisioned an internship program centered around campus ministry. While his plan didn't receive the funding for which he initially applied, it did get the attention of a task force of the Board of Ordained Ministry focused on recruiting young clergy.

"It was too good of an idea to let it just fall to the floor and not take shape," said Rev. Jonathan Smith, another South Georgia campus minister and a member of that task force.

The group pitched the plan to the St. Marys United Methodist Church Foundation of St. Marys, Georgia, received a $100,000 grant, and the Young Clergy Academy of the South Georgia Conference was born. Additional support came from the conference's Ministerial Education Fund and the New and Revitalized Congregational Development office.

The Young Clergy Academy each year offers nine-month internships to eight students in college or in their first or second year of seminary. A selected church (and, in some cases, a campus ministry) invests $2,500 toward an intern's $9,000 stipend. The investment is "something that we want to have in place so that churches take seriously the commitment they're making to the intern," Smith said. The Academy checks in monthly with interns and their supervising pastors, and provides retreats for the interns to spend time in theological reflection on their work.

"The goal is really for interns to catch a rhythm of life in the local church; more than just being the summer help," he said. "We wanted interns to really get a sense of what it's like to be in ministry on a day-to-day basis—interacting with the same group of people over a long period of time, shadowing ministers as they go about doing the business [of the church], and trying on ministry by teaching, preaching, leading groups, sitting in on meetings, and having a voice in those areas as well."

Longer internships also provide experience with finding balance in ministry. "If you're not able to balance the demands of the local church with the demands of your life, burnout happens very, very quickly," Smith said. "So there really was an emphasis on 'How we can make this an experience that's life-giving instead of draining, and helps those students and interns discover a healthy rhythm for ministry and life?'"

Smith says the task force also hopes to find ways to connect with students as young as fifth grade who might have a call to ministry. "If college football teams are looking at middle schoolers for potential all-stars, then we ought to be looking at our students who come to middle school retreat and high school retreat not as wonderful photo opportunities, but as the future leaders of our church, and even the present of our church, and find ways to help them connect with God's call on their life," he said. "The Young Clergy Academy is just one prong, one avenue for reaching out to young people."

THREE W'S OF PRINCIPLED LEADERSHIP

At Ginghamsburg, we have distilled many of the key leadership criteria into what we call the three W's: wisdom, work, and wealth. (The criteria were borrowed from my friend Len Sweet when I served under his leadership on the United Theological Seminary Board of Directors.) Each fall as our church identifies new Leadership Board candidates, those three W's are at the forefront. *Wisdom* implies that we seek folks who possess both earthly acumen and spiritual wisdom and discernment—people who are both proclaimers and practitioners of the faith. *Work* indicates that we only want to place folks in leadership who are actively engaged in serving the mission in some form of frontline ministry—in other words, a seat on the board should never be an individual's first or primary place of service. One advantage of this requirement is that it builds a diverse board that will include strong advocates and evangelists for their areas of ministry. *Wealth*, the final W, means that all board members are investing their earthly resources into the mission, a practice that Towers and Watson calls "proportional giving."

When we look across our congregations, if we can't identify the leaders we need, then we'd better be growing them. Jesus' disciples didn't enter his inner circle fully equipped to ignite a movement; they spent three intense years walking in the dust of the Rabbi Jesus to develop their leadership chops. Jesus' coaching of his disciples, sometimes described as the "show-and-tell" method, included these four classic steps:

1. I do, you watch.
2. I do, you help.
3. You do, I watch.
4. You do, with someone else learning from you.

And yet, even after a three-year "intensive" with Jesus, daily living the first three steps, the disciples hadn't completely nailed it. Otherwise, they would not have been cowering in the shadows while others visited the tomb after the crucifixion. It took a healthy dose of the Holy Spirit on the Day of Pentecost to put boots on the ground. Seeing their flawed example, we realize that discipleship is not an overnight venture; it is an investment of time, energy, and prayer for the long haul, and we had better get started before our graying clergy all die out.

CIRCLES, NOT ROWS

Within our churches, we must implement a strategy for moving the simply curious to the convinced and then to the committed. John Wesley faced the same struggle. He looked across the Anglican Church of his day and found leadership zeal for Christ lacking.

In his sermon "Scriptural Christianity," Wesley addressed "ye venerable men, who are more especially called to form the tender minds of youth, to dispel thence the shades of ignorance and error, and train them up to be wise unto salvation." He asked:

> Are you filled with the Holy Ghost? With all these fruits of the Spirit, which your important office so indispensably requires? Is your heart whole with God? Full of love and zeal to set up his kingdom on earth? Do you continually remind those under your care, that the one rational end of all our studies, is to know, love, and serve 'the only true God, and Jesus Christ, whom he hath sent?'...I fear it is not. Rather, have not pride and haughtiness of spirit, impatience and peevishness, sloth and indolence, gluttony and sensuality, and even a proverbial uselessness, been objected to us.[4]

After delivering this sermon, Wesley was barred from speaking in any university pulpit by his Oxford alma mater. Wesley came to the realization that he could not rely simply upon the seminaries and universities to grow the future leaders of the movement. All Jesus' followers would need to be discipled in the way of the cross and what it meant to live and serve in Christian community. This is how leaders of the movement would be identified and grown.

While Wesley was at Oxford, he and brother Charles joined some friends in the Holy Club, a small group who followed the practices of what Wesley referred to as the primitive and apostolic church. The Holy Club diligently practiced the disciplines of prayer, fasting, accountability, visits to the ill and imprisoned, regular Communion, and personal evangelizing. These disciplines were key elements in what Wesley perceived as four necessities for making and retaining disciples of Jesus Christ for the transformation of the world:

- Discipleship
- Small groups
- Lay leader development and deployment
- Holiness and service as the key discipleship goals

Wesley saw these activities being carried out in three groups: society, classes, and bands. He defined a *society*, or crowd, as a large group of people typically within a geographical area who would come together about once a week, much like a worship service today, to pray, sing, and study Scripture together. At this more corporate level, worshiping together could be significant, but deep discipleship was difficult.

Therefore, Wesley also organized *classes*, groups of twelve to twenty members of both genders who met one evening weekly under a trained leader. These sessions were more focused on confession, accountability, and a deeper understanding of the society's teaching. If you wanted to remain in a society, participation in a class was not optional.

The deepest discipleship happened within what Wesley called a *band*. A band would typically be only four people or so of the same gender who would meet weekly to answer with frankness some very hard questions, including, "What sins have you committed since the last meeting?" and "What temptations have you faced?" These bands often served as the training trenches for future discipleship leaders. Wesley understood, as Pastor Andy Stanley frequently notes, that something happens in circles that will never happen in rows.[5]

I will never underestimate the power that small groups exercised in my own ministry. When I arrived at Ginghamsburg thirty-six years ago, I found the typical small, family-controlled church. A core group of "godfathers" and "godmothers" within the church held tightly to all the reins and resources. However well intentioned those few folks may have been, their tight control wasn't healthy. Nothing will grow where new ideas are perpetually stifled. I knew that my first job would be to develop a new group or band of disciples whom I could help equip and empower to move the mission forward.

I let the controlling faction within that small church keep the only room that was available for an adult Sunday school class in the original building, while I set about identifying other people whose hearts, like John Wesley's, were "strangely warmed" by the call of Jesus. We met in our home, where we would study radical books such as Bonhoeffer's *The Cost of Discipleship* and Howard A. Snyder's *The Problem of Wineskins* and begin to dream new dreams. Soon, some of the Joshuas and Deborahs who had been meeting in my home began replacing existing committee members. Something happened in circles that didn't happen in rows.

John Ward was one of those Joshuas discipled in my home who helped to birth a movement. John started attending Ginghamsburg only three months after my appointment. His arrival at Ginghamsburg's little country chapel by State Highway 25A was in part a testimony to the power of invitation and the prompting of the Holy Spirit. John and his wife, Jeanne, were attenders of a church in a nearby community when Bob, an across-the-street neighbor, asked John about trying out his little country church with a new, young pastor. John gave the obligatory "Yeah, I will do that some time," then pushed it out of his mind as soon as he walked away. Then on the Sunday of Labor Day weekend, John woke up suddenly and told his startled wife, "Today we are going to that little church that Bob invited us to." Recently John, now age seventy, reminisced about that day.

> When Jeanne and I walked into the back of the sanctuary, it was chaos. People were greeting each other, laughing, and hugging—not our normal Sunday experience at the reserved church where we'd been attending. I looked around the room for my neighbor Bob and finally spotted him sitting head-down, appearing to pray in the midst of the fracas. He suddenly stopped, looked up, and spotted us, then pushed through the crowded room to throw his arms around me. He said, "I was just praying that you would be here, and God said yes. I looked up, and there you were."

John went on to say that "God started putting the pieces together for me all in that one weekend, and it was compelling."

After that first Sunday, I was privileged to witness John and Jeanne make an "all-in" commitment to Jesus. I knew that John was exactly the gifted type of leader Ginghamsburg needed to ignite a movement. Soon, he and Jeanne and a number of other couples were meeting in our home together, reading Bonhoeffer and Snyder, studying the birth of the church in Acts, pulling from Ephesians how the church is to function, and being schooled by 1 John in how we are to love.

All the people in that group became significant leaders at Ginghamsburg—witnesses to and evangelists for its explosive growth. John served on our board for multiple terms, helping us make the right Spirit-driven decisions. He taught our membership classes for twenty years, growing up new generations of disciples. When we were asked decades later to restore fading churches back to full health, John was my first choice for leading the teams that would till the soil and seed the crop.

In our recent conversation, John told me why revitalization at Ginghamsburg had succeeded:

> First, we realized that working together meant recognizing the worth and value of what God was doing in every individual, even when we didn't all agree. Next, we intentionally decided together that we would hear the Holy Spirit's voice, only doing and never failing to do what the Holy Spirit required. When we stumbled and got it wrong, we simply assumed we didn't hear the Spirit right and would go back to prayer.

John hasn't lost the fire in his gut. Eyes gleaming, he ended our conversation by saying, "When someone realizes how the Holy Spirit can use them to change the world, they will storm the gates of hell in Jesus' name. I know. I saw it."

Ginghamsburg remains focused on empowering leaders who empower others in the twenty-first century. We have got to be about identifying and investing in the next generation of

CHRISTMAS INSTITUTE
(PHILIPPINES)

Christmas Institute is a five-day Christian retreat for youth and young adults from middle school up to college, facilitated by The United Methodist Church. The program, held December 26–30 every year, has been so successful that many Filipino United Methodist congregations in the United States also offer it.

"Christmas Institute is an all-in avenue for youngsters to experience the redeeming grace of God through faith in Jesus for self-transformation," says Kevin John Maddela, a youth leader from Solano United Methodist in the province of Nueva Vizcaya, Philippines. This year will be his eleventh year at the retreat.

Christmas Institute offers all the excitement of a summer camp and a church lock-in. There's time for recreation, Bible study, and leadership development workshops. Christmas Institute is a youth-led gathering that gives young people experience as lay leaders. The programming is prepared by older participants for the younger ones with guidance from pastors, deacons, and lay leaders.

April Gonzaga-Mercado is another veteran of the Christmas Institute. She says she always enjoyed the time away, surrounded by peers who shared her faith. "Having fellow Christians in the same age bracket allowed me to be open about my struggles as a teenager where we can relate with and pray for each other."

At Christmas Institute, Mercado honed her talents in communications and creative arts. The experience led to her present career in communications. Mercado is a special projects manager and field representative for United Methodist Communications in the Philippines.

Another enthusiastic former participant of the program is Rev. MarLu Primero Scott, who answered a call late in life to go to seminary and become a pastor. She has served as pastor at Wilbur Memorial United Methodist in Washington State and as chaplain at Union Theological Seminary in Cavite, Philippines. The seeds of her second career in ministry were planted in the mid-1960s while attending Christmas Institute at Muzon Methodist Episcopal Church in the Philippines. "It was during one of those services that I committed my life to God, uncertain of where it was going to take me."

Primero Scott remembers fondly the feeling of adventure as teenage participants would give up the comforts of home to sleep on the floor of a church for the week. "Every delegate had to secure sleeping space they shared with fifty-plus other youth. Everyone brought a blanket, a mat, a mosquito net, and a pillow. Each had to bring their Bible and a notebook to take notes for reporting back home."

Across the Philippines, up to fifteen thousand young people attend Christmas Institute in a given year. Many pastors and lay leaders will tell you that their time at Christmas Institute led to their calling to serve the church.

"Memories of Christmas Institutes continue to stoke the fire of the person I am today," says Primero Scott.

Adapted from an article by Lilla Marigza on UMC.org
(Courtesy: United Methodist Communications)

principled leaders, not taking orders from those who have settled into the comfortable status quo.

What John Wesley recognized in his three-strand approach of society, class, and band is that you don't need ordained clergy to lead a movement; you simply need deeply discipled, gifted, and anointed leaders. I greatly value my formal seminary training, but some of the very best faith leaders I know never finished college.

The next mission of Jesus to reach the world isn't happening in the seminary or in sanctuary seats, but in the streets. Who are you discipling? Who are they discipling? What are we "showing"? How are we "telling"? The measure of effectiveness for a church is not its seating capacity, but its sending capacity.

BURNING BUSHES AND LIVING LETTERS

One key first step with our current congregations is to help our folks identify their passions. I talk about this in my book *Dare to Dream* (Abingdon Press, 2013). What do people like to do so much that they would be willing to do it for free? What "burning bushes" have they encountered, where we as current leaders simply need to throw on some kerosene and watch the flames? Oftentimes I find that people discover their mission and call simply by stepping out to serve when the opportunity presents itself. If Dr. Harry Whitehouse had not called me when I was in college and asked me to help with the church youth group, or if I had not responded to the call, I never would have discovered my passion for working with teens. Student ministry in turn revealed to me a passion for leading and teaching, as well as a lasting call to local church ministry, a call I am still living out more than four decades later.

How are you building people into doers and not simply hearers of the word? In his second letter to the Corinthians, Paul writes:

> You yourselves are our letter, written on our hearts, known and read by everyone. You show that you are a letter from Christ, the result of our ministry, written not with ink but with the Spirit of the living God, not on tablets of stone but on tablets of human hearts. (2 Corinthians 3:2-3)

In many ways I am a letter written by Dr. Whitehouse. I am also a result of the ministry of Mrs. Cook. Mrs. Cook represented a place of safety in the neighborhood where I grew up, the house you could visit for a fresh cookie and a little love when there was nowhere else to go. It was Mrs. Cook who told me long before I knew it myself that God would be calling me to be either a doctor or a pastor. She would not have been surprised to learn that I am a pastor and my son is a surgeon. I am the product of godly, principled Christian leaders who believed in me, invested in me, and spoke hope into my life. Dr. Whitehouse and Mrs. Cook were just two of many who demonstrated a better way, challenging me to turn my life into a lifelong psalm of ascent.

On my recent John Wesley tour in England, one of several sharp United Methodist pastors I was privileged to meet was Mike Schreiner, lead pastor of Morning Star Church in Dardenne Prairie, Missouri. Mike founded the church in 1999, originally leading a group of about two hundred people in a banquet center. Morning Star now averages about two thousand in attendance. Mike is high-energy and admits he is someone with the ability to "make coffee nervous." Mike is also sold on the importance of making disciples of Jesus Christ for the transformation of the world. To accomplish this, Mike is a proponent of repeatable processes and thinks in terms of steps, not programs. Like John Wesley, Mike believes that "the only way to keep Methodists alive is to keep them moving."[6]

Morning Star has identified four paths that take folks deeper into faith, only to then launch them out into mission. The paths are discipleship, leadership, giving, and serving. Each path has clearly defined steps offering easily accessible classes and multiple on-ramps. The paths create a common DNA and language that marry the church's mission with the paths' curriculum and the people being discipled.

Mike indicates that the "secret sauce" for the discipleship and leadership paths is the step called Connect Coaches. For the discipleship path, everyone who finishes is assigned a connect coach, who meets with the graduate to review that person's ministry profile and spiritual gifts and to hear the individual's faith story. The coach will help identify two to four initial service opportunities and a ministry or small group in which the individual might thrive.

Mike refers to leadership as "discipleship on steroids." Each person finishing the leadership path is assigned a more specialized coach to partner with for the next steps and continuing growth. If a new leader is called to children's ministry, a children's coach will be assigned—a seasoned, discipled, and discipling leader who will ensure fruitful ministry. Leaders are trained in how to identify, mentor, and multiply new leaders.

As Mike describes it, a true leader believes that "our fruit grows on other people's trees."

GETTING IT DONE

God isn't dead; we just have allowed his church to be. There is a better way. Let's pull out all the stops, set aside excuses, and invest whatever is required to develop principled Christian leaders. It can and will happen. John Ward, Mike Schreiner, Dr. Whitehouse, Mrs. Cook, and countless others are proof.

A Few Ideas for Getting Started

- If you don't already have a small group ministry within your church, now is the time to start. Something happens in circles that doesn't happen in rows. Study of Scripture, prayer, accountability, and care for one another are key components of a vibrant small group community.

- If you are a pastor or seasoned church leader, identify those within the congregation whose hearts are strangely warmed and invite them into your own home for deeper discipling and mentoring.

- Does your church have clearly defined discipleship and leadership paths with easily understood steps and multiple access points? (Some good access points are guest orientation, membership process, classes for deeper spiritual growth, small groups, and service opportunities including some that fall outside traditional ministry roles, such as greeting in worship or serving with children.) How will you make a point of converting the crowd into convicted and active followers of Jesus?

- Ensure that you have included in your own circle both those who are ahead of you spiritually and those who are behind. Who is coaching you? Whom are you coaching? Intentionality is important. Who is asking you the hard questions?

- At Ginghamsburg, we use the word servant instead of volunteer. Volunteer is institutional language implying that there is a choice of when, how, and if to serve based on personal convenience. Jesus came to serve, not to be served (Mark 10:45). Does your church culture proclaim and model service as a Kingdom priority? You get what you expect and what you celebrate as priorities. Call is important, but many folks find their call during service, not before.

- How are you helping teens and college-age students in your congregation be alert to the call of God into ministry, whether as a layperson or as someone trained for the vocation? How are you connecting students into programs, internships, and ministry opportunities that will help them explore and grow?

2
Engaging in Ministry with the Poor

He speaks, and listening to his voice, new life the dead receive;
the mournful, broken hearts rejoice, the humble poor believe.
  —Charles Wesley, "O For a Thousand Tongues to Sing"

GOSPEL (NOUN): GOOD NEWS TO THE POOR

In his hometown of Nazareth, Jesus announced his mission statement by quoting Isaiah. Notice that of all the groups Jesus named, the poor got top billing.

> "The Spirit of the Lord is on me,
>   because he has anointed me
>   to proclaim good news to the poor.

> He has sent me to proclaim freedom for the prisoners
> > and recovery of sight for the blind,
> to set the oppressed free,
> > to proclaim the year of the Lord's favor."
> > > (Luke 4:18-19)

Christian means "little Christ." If proclaiming good news to the poor is Christ's priority, then it must be a priority of ours.

All around the world people have an unfulfilled hunger for food and for meaningful relationships. The church is uniquely positioned to help people meet both needs. More than two thousand years ago Jesus said, "You will always have the poor among you" (John 12:8). Jesus walked, lived, and ministered among the poor, and we do too—yet we oftentimes overlook or ignore Jesus' first priority.

The World Bank reported in October 2015 that the world had achieved the United Nations' "first Millennium Development Goal target—to cut the 1990 poverty rate in half by 2015—five years ahead of schedule, in 2010." The report then soberly added: "Despite this progress, the number of people living in extreme poverty globally remains unacceptably high." According to the most recent estimates, in 2012, 12.7 percent of the world's population lived at or below $1.90 a day in 2012. That means 896 million people lived on less than $1.90 a day. At higher poverty lines, the numbers are worse—over 2.1 billion people in the developing world lived on less than $3.10 a day.[1]

To bring this reality closer to home for some of us, the US Census Bureau reports that the US poverty rate in 2014 for children under age eighteen was 21.1 percent. That's more than one in five of our kids.[2] Right here in my own local area, Ohio ranks third in the nation for states with the lowest food security, and Dayton, where two of our campuses are located, is the fourth hungriest city in America in terms of food hardship, according to the Food Research and Action Center.[3]

In light of these shocking statistics, I don't believe when it comes to poverty that Jesus is ready to pat his church on the back just yet and say, "Well done, good and faithful servant." We ought to give thanks for the decrease in global poverty while never ceasing Jesus' mission.

Just before his ascension back to the Father's side, Jesus' assignment to his followers was clear:

> "All authority in heaven and on earth has been given to me. Therefore go and make disciples of all nations, baptizing them in the name of the Father and of the Son and of the Holy Spirit, and teaching them to obey everything I have commanded you. And surely I am with you always, to the very end of the age" (Matthew 28:18-20).

Within The United Methodist Church, we have encapsulated that commission into a spot-on mission statement: "To make disciples of Jesus Christ for the transformation of the world."

Some might argue that neither the Great Commission nor the United Methodist mission statement says anything about the poor. But "to make disciples" means developing and deploying Jesus followers who will implement God's kingdom vision and mission on planet earth. Our desire to bring people to Jesus is critical, but we must first provide what they need to maintain life. The Epistle of James, one of my favorite books in the Bible, addresses this clearly:

> Suppose a brother or a sister is without clothes and daily food. If one of you says to them, "Go in peace; keep warm and well fed," but does nothing about their physical needs, what good is it? In the same way, faith by itself, if it is not accompanied by action, is dead. (James 2:15-17)

From "Ministry To" to "Ministry With"

In 2002, Rev. Owen Ross moved into a low-income, high-immigrant area of Dallas, got to know his neighbors, offered social services, and shepherded two discipleship groups into existence. On Ash Wednesday 2003, La Fundición de Cristo—Christ's Foundry United Methodist Mission—held its first worship service, with twenty-two people attending.

Twelve years later, weekly worship attendance at Christ's Foundry had climbed to about 225 people, with one service in Spanish and the other bilingual.

"Doing ministry with low-income people was different," Ross says. Though he had learned Spanish as a Peace Corps volunteer in Ecuador, he discovered knowledge gaps. For example, he didn't know the Spanish word for "mercy."

"I had always operated from a high-income context, in which social services were the basis of our ministry to the poor," he said. "I found out that starting with social services is not the way to do ministry with the poor."

Because outside funding is necessary when congregants have limited resources, other congregations became "covenant churches," supporting the ministry with financial and relational resources.

"Building, maintaining, and developing those peer relationships with higher-income communities is what has enabled our financial success," Ross says. Christ's Foundry has found it essential to have a staff member dedicated to maintaining covenant partner relationships.

That dedicated staff person is as crucial now as ever, because as the mission gains more participating community members, the covenant relationships change. As the community of faith has come into its own, people from covenant churches have fewer opportunities to participate.

"We continue to explore, OK, what are ways in which we can build mutually transforming peer relationships between higher income and lower income people when everything around them tells them that they are not peers?" Ross says.

Christ's Foundry guards against anchoring ministry in social services, he adds, "especially those social services that reiterate the lie of the world that some of us are superior and others are inferior."

Whenever Christ's Foundry distributes goods or services, its community members—peers of the recipients—invite recipients to help distribute services and to participate in congregational life. "All of our food ministries today are completely run by the community, and so when community members come to receive, they see their neighbors providing the food and inviting them to assist in providing the service, as well as to come to worship or to their small groups with them," Ross says.

"I feel the church has typically seen the poor as recipients of social services rather than as full brothers and sisters in Christ: being eager to share cans of soup with them, but slow to share Sunday school with them; eager to invite them to an English class or receive school supplies, but slow to invite them to worship or to adjust the worship service in a way that would be appealing," he says. "Neither Jesus nor John Wesley divorced social services from religious services. They were integrated and holistic. I believe true ministry with the poor is holistic and integrated ministry."

This is why since 2005 Ginghamsburg Church has invested millions of dollars into sustainable humanitarian projects in Darfur, Sudan, a Muslim state where proselytizing not only puts the evangelist's life at risk but also the lives of those being helped. The gospel is to be good news for all, not just for those we preach to.

When I was working on my undergraduate degree in social work at the University of Cincinnati, I learned about Abraham Maslow's hierarchy of needs. Maslow, an American psychology professor building on the work of others, began to research what it took to become a fully self-actualized human being. From his research Maslow derived a hierarchy, identifying a series of needs people need to have met before they can reach their full potential. On the first rung were physiological needs such as food and water. Next were needs for safety, including physical safety, employment, and resources. Maslow believed that until a person feels those items are secured, it is very difficult to fulfill the person's higher needs pertaining to love, esteem, and self-actualization. Others in the field have since refuted some of Maslow's findings, but almost all agree that it is difficult for people to reach the pinnacle of their potential when they are hungry, thirsty, afraid, or not sure how they are going to feed their crying baby.[4]

Starving people certainly are not barred from finding Jesus, but extreme poverty and hunger are a barrier. For such people, believing in a loving God of provision and grace is difficult when those who identify themselves by his name demonstrate so little interest in the urgent needs of God's children all around them.

A KINGDOM PRIORITY

Bringing good news to the poor didn't just materialize in the New Testament with Jesus' declaration in Nazareth. Throughout the Old Testament, God's people are directed to care for the poor, widowed, and orphaned. In the Book of Deuteronomy, Moses instructed the people just before his death about their responsibility to the poor:

> If anyone is poor among your fellow Israelites in any of the towns of the land the Lord your God is giving you, do not be hardhearted or tightfisted toward them. Rather, be open-handed and freely lend them whatever they need.
>
> (Deuteronomy 15:7-8)

Later in Deuteronomy, Moses described in practical terms how the poor would be fed:

> When you are harvesting in your field and you overlook a sheaf, do not go back to get it. Leave it for the foreigner, the fatherless and the widow, so that the Lord your God may bless you in all the work of your hands. When you beat the olives from your trees, do not go over the branches a second time.... When you harvest the grapes in your vineyard, do not go over the vines again. Leave what remains for the foreigner, the fatherless and the widow.
>
> (Deuteronomy 24:19-21)

Note that the leftover crops and produce left on the margins were to be gleaned by those in need of food, not simply bagged up and breezily handed over by generous benefactors. True ministry with the poor is about a "we're in this together" community partnership, not about a more privileged class doling out largesse to those in need. We will revisit this topic in a moment.

The psalmists frequently describe God's special relationship with the poor:

- "Because the poor are plundered and the needy groan, / I will now arise," says the LORD. / "I will protect them from those who malign them." (Psalm 12:5)
- "Who is like you, LORD? / You rescue the poor from those too strong for them, / the poor and needy from those who rob them." (Psalm 35:10)
- This poor man called, and the LORD heard him; / he saved him out of all his troubles. (Psalm 34:6)

These are only three of the more than 440 uses in the Bible of the words *poor* or *needy*.[5]

Justice for all people is a significant theme throughout Scripture. Isaiah declares, "For I, the Lord, love justice" and reminds us that "the Sovereign Lord will make righteousness and praise spring up before all nations" (Isaiah 61:8, 11). Ministry with the poor is a matter of justice.

Years ago, author Philip Yancey asked in his book, *The Jesus I Never Knew*, why God is partial to the poor and disadvantaged. He got his answer in part from Catholic nun Monika Hellwig, who had identified advantages unique to the poor. In short, the poor understand that they urgently need redemption and recognize their reliance on God, other people, and each another. The poor do not exaggerate their own importance, and they see the advantages of cooperation over competition. Perhaps most importantly, the gospel actually sounds like good news to them.[6] Those of us who do not recognize our own reliance on God suffer from the poverty of complacency and have much to learn from the poor. This is why our ministry must be *with* the poor and not *for* the poor. We learn from one another about the nature of God and what it means to live life abundantly.

I have to admit there's a personal reason why I am so convicted about ministry with the poor. As I frequently remind my Ginghamsburg congregation, I am in my mid-sixties and almost dead. That means that the content of my life on which I will be assessed during my final exam with Jesus is almost fully complete! That means it's almost time for me to turn in my blue exam book, for those of you old enough to remember what that is. God may be the God of the do-overs, but there is no do-over after you are dead. The rich man discovered this in Jesus' parable about Lazarus, the poor beggar in Luke 16 whose needs were completely ignored by the rich man until it was too late.

To me there is no real mystery as to what will happen on the Day of Judgment. Jesus spells it out clearly:

> "When the Son of Man comes in his glory, and all the angels with him, he will sit on his glorious throne. All the nations will be gathered before him, and he will separate the people one from another as a shepherd separates the sheep from the goats. He will put the sheep on his right and the goats on his left." (Matthew 25:31-33)

As Jesus followers, we definitely want to find ourselves in the sheep column, among those who will inherit "the kingdom prepared for you since the creation of the world" (v. 34), because we gave encouragement and sustenance to the hungry, thirsty, homeless, naked, ill, and imprisoned. Conversely, the goats among us, who have ignored the needs and cries of the least and the lost, will be sent away from Jesus' presence forever and into eternal punishment.

Jesus never directs us to do what he himself did not sacrificially model, declaring to his disciples after cleaning their filthy feet after his final supper, "I am among you as one who serves" (Luke 22:27). We are most like Jesus when we serve others.

FROM THE BEGINNING

John Wesley, founder of the Wesleyan movement, completely understood Jesus' call to care for the least of these and did not limit the geographic scope of those he felt called to serve. In the early days of the Wesleyan revival, John found himself in conflict with the Anglican Bishop of Bristol, Dr. Joseph Butler. One of the biggest points of contention was Wesley's propensity for preaching in the parishes of other Anglican clergy without first asking permission. After one stern warning from the bishop, Wesley replied, "My Lord, my business on earth is to do what good I can. Wherever therefore I think I can do most good, there I must stay as long as I think so. At present, I think I can do the most good here. Therefore, here I stay." Today we often reinterpret Wesley's statement as "Do all the good you can. By all the means you can. In all the ways you can. In all the places you can." This reflects the start of "the world is my parish" theology that undergirds the Methodist itinerant system.[7]

Wesley took his own responsibility for the poor very seriously. While a fellow at Lincoln College, Oxford, even though his income was just thirty pounds per year, Wesley discovered by living frugally that he could survive on twenty-eight pounds per year, freeing up two pounds to give to the poor. He still managed to live on twenty-eight pounds in the subsequent year, even though his income doubled, freeing up thirty-two pounds for the poor. In the third year, by keeping his living expense the same, his new income of ninety pounds gave him sixty-two pounds for ministry with the poor.[8] Wesley didn't simply preach it; he lived it. Frugality and the generosity it empowered became lifelong practices.

Wesley felt special empathy for coal miners, who were members of a filthy, thankless, dangerous profession and were outcasts even among other poor people. Wesley also frequently ministered to inmates in workhouses and prisons, including those condemned to death. Children and soldiers also held a special place in Wesley's heart.[9]

Wesley's Methodist Societies fed and clothed those in need and provided a safe refuge for travelers and people fleeing persecution. Societies created dispensaries for medicine and established orphanages and free schools for the poor. Microfinance loans were made without interest so the poor could begin small-business start-ups and pull themselves out of poverty. Many of these ministries were funded in part by the working poor themselves, who in turn were serving other poor neighbors.[10]

Wesley's famous sermon on "The Use of Money" was delivered in 1744 and contained his three key principles for money management: "Gain [earn] all you can, save all you can, and give all you can."[11] Wesley did not just preach those principles; he lived them.

John's brother Charles, a lifelong partner in ministry and a prolific hymn writer, penned these words, which encapsulate the Wesleys' concern for the poor:

> The poor as Jesus' bosom-friends,
> The poor he makes his latest care.

GRACE-DRIVEN OUTREACH
CREATES DIVERSE COMMUNITY

In 1999, a group of churches rented a storefront in Columbus, Ohio, and opened the United Methodist Free Store as a way to focus on a common mission.

"There are no eligibility requirements, everything is always free, and it's about radical hospitality," says Rev. John Edgar. "That's where we form relationships."

They formed so many relationships, in fact, that the Free Store led to the 2002 founding of Church for All People, where Edgar serves as senior pastor. In addition to racial diversity (like its neighborhood, the church is about half Caucasian, half African American), economic diversity makes Church for All People unique: about two-thirds of its worshiping community live below the poverty line.

"For us, what matters is do I get to know the name of that person, and do I share my name with that person?" Edgar says. "Do I slow down long enough to hear somebody's story, and do I share part of my story? Am I listening, and am I vulnerable? Not only do I pray for you, but do I invite you to pray for me—do I believe your prayers are equally heard and efficacious? We build relationships of mutuality."

Sunday worship at Church for All People includes a variety of music styles and a lot of time for spoken prayer requests.

"The longest segment in worship is sharing of joys and of sorrows," Edgar says. "There's a lot of testimony, most of which is incredibly raw and vulnerable...that becomes the defining center energy in worship for us."

Worship also happens on weekdays, about a half-hour before the Free Store opens for business.

"Everything is free in the Free Store because we want people to literally—not figuratively, but literally—touch grace," he says. "We preach that today you will shop in a store and you will touch God's grace. You will go up to a checkout counter, and they will put God's grace in a bag, you'll carry it home with you on the bus, and tomorrow morning you will clothe yourself in God's grace. And that's the gospel we preach. That's why it's free."

The church walks alongside people to help them leave poverty behind, employing the concept of asset-based community development.

"From a faith-based perspective, there are two assets that never go away: the presence of God's Spirit if we're lined up with what God's trying to do, and the people themselves made in God's image," Edgar says.

Through listening to their hopes and dreams, the church has helped community members move from near-homelessness to being homeowners. And starting with one vacant duplex in 2005, they have made available hundreds of homes, amounting to $50 million of affordable housing in Columbus.

Edgar acknowledges that building a diverse community of faith has its challenges.

"Everybody was thrilled, particularly the hard-living marginalized folks, that this was a church where they were truly welcome, and where we'd gone out of our way to convince them, 'If you come, we will treat you with utmost respect.' And that worked the first week. And by the second week . . . we discovered that a whole lot of these people had no desire to tolerate each other. . . . In some ways, it was just this bad comedy about all kinds of marginalized people saying, 'I'm glad I'm here, but you can't let *them* in.' So we've spent a lot of time establishing the core ethos that, no, it's a church for all people.

"We actually use the exact same call to worship every single week: 'God's love is deep and wide, and God loves us just the way we are.' And then there's also the core affirmation of the church, that everybody in the church has memorized. It's real simple. It just says, 'God loves you just the way you are. God is not finished with you yet.'"

> To all his followers' commands,
> And wills us with our hands to bear;
> The poor our dearest care we make,
> And love them for our Savior's sake.[12]

The Wesleys understood that true Christians had to care vitally about both the spiritual and physical well-being of people. John and Charles were committed to "doing all the good we can...to the bodies and souls of men" and never lost focus on pursuing not only souls for Jesus but also social equality and economic justice.[13] They remained cognizant of God's seemingly preferential concern for the poor expressed throughout Scripture.

STARTING FROM SCRATCH

When I first arrived at the little self-focused country church of Ginghamsburg, I quickly recognized that my challenge would be to convert the congregation's consumer mind-set to one that was focused on producing God's blessings within the lives of others. I taught a series of sermons on the Book of Acts to model taking the church into the world, not just coaxing the unchurched into worship. (Note that it's called the Book of *Acts*, not the Book of Beliefs!)

We did invite others to join us inside the walls, but we were inclusive about it. I still remember how concerned my trustees were when I proposed that Alcoholics Anonymous use our sanctuary as a meeting space—especially since AA in that era required that facilities allow smoking. They finally agreed, and each Sunday I felt the presence of Jesus as I stared at the cigarette burns in the carpet.

Church members began to catch the vision of what it meant to live and serve like Jesus. Peggy began a gently used clothing store. Sue started a food pantry. Dean directed our visitation and hospital teams, and Tom organized our mission teams. Rose led the prayer chain. My job was simply to pour a little kerosene on their burning bushes.

As the church grew, so did the outreach. Over time, Ginghamsburg would birth three 501(c)(3) organizations that now serve nearly sixty thousand of our neighbors annually. By creating 501(c)(3) nonprofits, we gained access to funding sources not typically available to churches and were able to multiply exponentially what we accomplished in ministry with the poor. However, we don't use those funding sources as an excuse for abdicating our own missional calling as a church. We continue to provide part of the financial support, most of the servant hands and feet, and the majority of the facility needs for our outreach organizations.

New Creation Counseling Center was founded in 1993 on the principle that professional counseling should be available to the entire community, even if a person cannot afford the full cost of care. Although the center accepts insurance, it has implemented a sliding fee schedule based on income and ability to pay, so that no one needing services is left behind. New Creation provides more than 970 clinical counseling sessions to 2,200-plus clients each year, covering approximately $394,000 in uncompensated care annually.

Our original Ginghamsburg food pantry, which started in a basement closet in the two-room country church during the mid-1970s, was the genesis of our New Path 501(c)(3) outreach arm. New Path's material assistance and life development programs now serve fifty-seven thousand of our neighbors each year.

New Path provides food, repaired and refurbished vehicles, clothing, furniture, medical equipment and supplies, pet food, and more, helping to meet material needs across Miami and Montgomery Counties in Ohio.

Many of our material assistance ministries also have a built-in "learn-earn-serve" component. For example, people don't receive repaired and refurbished vehicles until they have completed life skills training, proven they have enough income for car fuel and maintenance, and served alongside other New Path servants to give back to those in need around them. In addition to material assistance, New Path gives folks a hand up and a new lease on life through GED programs and employment-skill training. The greatest win we can have is to help a family escape the generational trap of poverty, giving the children of our struggling neighbors some new life-pictures of what their future can be.

Clubhouse is our after-school, teen-led mentoring and tutoring program that serves at-risk children in six communities located near our three worshiping campuses. Each year, Clubhouse holds 120 sessions for more than 450 children through the efforts of 400 trained teens and 85 adults.

Like John Wesley, the people of Ginghamsburg Church believe that our parish is the world and not just our backyard communities. In fall of 2004, the Holy Spirit prompted the church to intervene in the first genocide of the twenty-first century that was unfolding in Darfur, Sudan. Our rallying cry that Advent season—"Christmas is not your birthday"—resulted in the church family bringing in $317,000 to fund the United Methodist Committee on Relief's first foray into Sudan and to implement a sustainable agricultural program that fed 5,209 households. More than a decade later we are still challenging ourselves to bring in an equal amount at Christmas as we spend on ourselves for ministry with the poor. Over that time more than $8 million has been invested into projects that are sustaining and empowering tens of thousands of lives.

START SMALL—BUT START

I believe many of us want to do more than we are doing, but we fail to act. I blame part of that inaction on our dangerous scarcity mentality: "There is only so much to go around, and I need to ensure that my family (my church, my community, my country, my ethnicity, those people who look and act most like I do) gets first dibs." How quickly we seem to lose trust in a Father who has "cattle on a thousand hills" (Psalm 50:10). This scarcity mentality is in part what drives factions within the United States to long for large, patrolled walls that divide the "haves" from the "have nots." We mistakenly buy into the false prophecy that building walls will make us safer than building essential relationships—and trust. The Apostle Paul declares that Christ "himself is our peace" who has "destroyed the barrier, the dividing wall of hostility" (Ephesians 2:14). Christ calls us to tear down walls, not build them!

Some readers may have "yes, but" thoughts running through their minds that get in the way of doing ministry with the poor. "Yes, you can do all those wonderful 'ministry with the poor' initiatives and nonprofits, but you are Ginghamsburg/large/rich/crazy"—or some other adjective of your choice. I hear that. Yet when I first laid eyes on Ginghamsburg, it was a church of fewer than one hundred people with a budget of $27,000 a year. When you have the resources of God's kingdom at your disposal, size and budget are never barriers.

One of our newest and most favorite ministries emerged this past summer, simply called the "Bologna Brigade." Jason, a member of Ginghamsburg's maintenance team, watched a video on Facebook about a simple sandwich ministry in Minnesota that was impacting the lives of hungry children. Jason could not get the story out of his head. He approached Bill, the executive director of our New Path 501(c)(3), who felt compelled to help Jason bring his God-nudging to reality. Bill took the vision to the Salvation Army where he serves on the board of directors in Piqua, Ohio, one of our neighboring communities.

Hundreds of students in Piqua qualify for free or reduced meals during the school year. When summer vacation starts, however, families often struggle to afford three meals a day. The Salvation Army steps in to offer free summer meals to Piqua children between the ages of one and eighteen. There's no registration, no paperwork, and no cost for the children. To receive a hot meal Monday through Friday, the kids simply need to show up at one of the seven designated stops in neighborhoods, church parking lots, and parks.

Bill and Jason decided to assist these children, who already were being served by the Salvation Army on weekdays, by providing bologna sandwiches for the weekend. Jason and a team of servants, calling themselves the Bologna Brigade, would meet in the church kitchen each Friday morning to assemble sandwiches. Then they would hit the streets, following the Salvation Army mobile canteen around Piqua in a Ginghamsburg van. Approximately three hundred sandwiches were handed out each week to ensure that kids had weekend lunch. Each sandwich cost $.37, which added up to about $110 per week. Now, a small church may not gather $317,000 for an agricultural program in the Sudan, but how many could invest $100 a week to feed lunch to some hungry children?

Of course, the next step in the Bologna Brigade will be to connect the children served bologna with the opportunity and training to "serve the bologna"—whether literally or figuratively through other acts of service—so that this "hand-out" ministry is transformed into a "giving back" opportunity for the hungry kids.

More on Ministry with, Not Ministry For

I am frequently blessed by stories of amazing things that churches accomplish when the saints remember that they serve and trust a God of abundance, not scarcity. I recently received this e-mail from a pastor named Ali Petrey:

> I'm the Associate Pastor of Congregational Discipleship at Lima Trinity United Methodist Church. We are an older congregation in the heart of Lima, Ohio, a rust-belt Midwest town of about 34,000 residents. Although industrial and healthcare jobs are available in the area, our church's downtown neighborhood has a poverty rate of thirty-four percent. Our worship attendance ranges from 120 to 180 on a Sunday, and we also serve approximately 150 neighbors breakfast each Sunday.

Ali went on to add that Trinity houses a Churches United Pantry (CUP) and offices for a rotating family shelter, hosts a free store on its campus as well as one in the community in partnership with other churches, provides school supplies for children starting school, and offers summer literacy programs. The e-mail concluded:

> Most importantly we have brought in members who came to us through these outreach programs. They have been baptized, counseled, taken their covenantal vows, and

GIVE THE HELPING HAND
(RUSSIA)

"Give the Helping Hand" is the name of a ministry that started at Samara United Methodist Church three years ago.

The council of leaders organized the ministry for several reasons. One reason was that our church is situated in a district with adverse influences, where there are dysfunctional families and people who are disabled and sick, as well as newly released prisoners and those with substance dependencies.

In addition, the ministry would raise and improve awareness of the church, as there is a negative perception in Samara of Protestant churches. Locals don't trust Protestants, and there are biases and stereotypes. The ministry would provide a unique opportunity to preach the good news, including through films, music, personal talks, and counseling. Finally, the ministry would provide a chance to help those who need rehabilitation and can join one of the rehabilitation centers.

Thanks to this ministry, many community members for the first time got to know a Protestant church by meeting ministers and community members in person. Some of the people visited the church for special occasions then became a part of the church. Some were helped to join a rehabilitation program. As people experienced our care, compassion, and love, their prejudices about the church vanished.

Nowadays the program is a well-functioning ministry. It is particularly important that the parish members are taking part in it. People cook the food, make donations, and serve others by giving away food and helping the guests. We have learned that many are in need of clothes, particularly during the winter months, so we started collecting clothes and giving them away.

The ministry united the people and gave our community a new purpose. We spend a lot of time and resources on the ministry, but we also receive much. We feel God's blessings flowing through the ministry.

Once we started the ministry, we realized that God is supporting us and blessing us in other things too. We discovered new leaders, who began to serve regularly.... For instance, Elena Lipatova has started to lead the Give the Helping Hand. She pours a lot of care and energy into the ministry. She gives her heart, and the ministry in turn has brought spiritual growth and changes in her life

This year we received help from United Methodist Church in Eurasia, so we now have a device for air disinfection, which we use in the rooms where the ministry takes place. Because of this new blessing, we do not have to worry about the spread of infection among the people who come to eat or those who serve food.

We are grateful for those who supported our congregation. God bless.

—Olga Ganina, translated by Maxim Kvyatkovskiy

more. They are ushers, acolytes, and in leadership in the breakfast service and free store. Some have finished their education and are now gaining practical experience in internships.

As Ali notes, ministry with the poor means empowering the poor to produce fruit, both for themselves and for the Kingdom.

When we examine Jesus' miracles, we see that Jesus consistently invited others into the miracle-making process, whether to serve their own needs or enhance the larger community. The disciples, on first meeting Jesus in Luke 5, had an amazing catch of fish after a frustrating overnight failure, but only after following Jesus' directive to recast their freshly washed nets. Jesus fed the five thousand because a little boy sacrificed his packed lunch. The paralyzed man in Matthew 9 was healed but still had to pick up his mat and walk. The blind man in John 9 was required to wash his eyes in the Pool of Siloam. Jesus healed another physically disabled man only after his friends went to the trouble of carrying him up to and lowering him down through the roof of the house where Jesus was teaching. And perhaps Christ's most astounding miracle—raising Lazarus from the dead—wasn't complete until Lazarus's friends and neighbors rolled away the stone blocking the tomb (John 11:39) and unwrapped Lazarus' burial cloths (John 11:44). Even Jesus' first documented miracle, the transformation of water into wine for the marriage of Cana, required the servants for the wedding party to fill large water jars first (John 2:7). We are all in this together—with Christ!

Often it is tempting for middle-class Jesus followers to perceive ourselves as shining knights on white steeds, galloping into troubled places to rescue hapless paupers. Ministry with the poor, though, requires the recognition that "we are you" and "you are us." All of us, regardless of economic status, have the call and the giftedness to be producers of God's blessings in the lives of others, not simply consumers of stuff.

Our New Path car ministry is a great example of ministry with the poor instead of ministry for the poor. It's a ministry about empowering people, not simply handing out stuff. To earn a repaired vehicle, recipients first must learn by attending an orientation session, three training sessions called "More Month Than Money," and a basic car maintenance class. After learning and earning, each program participant then spends a required number of hours "paying it forward" by serving alongside the rest of our New Path team.

Maria, one New Path car recipient, had found herself financially unable to purchase another vehicle when her previous automobile stopped running and was beyond reasonable repair. She received a car from New Path after completing the required learn–earn–serve components. Inspired by the "More Month than Money" classes, she is now saving money and on track to purchase another vehicle in two years. Maria then intends to return the New Path car, making it available to the next person in need of reliable transportation. Even though her service requirements were long ago met, Maria has remained active in serving with New Path, and she is often overheard encouraging other car program participants to continue to serve with New Path after earning a vehicle.

Jim and Kathi Sitzman, two longtime Ginghamsburg members who have served in the car ministry since its inception, are spiritual shepherds to those in the program, offering prayer, withholding judgment, and providing both day-to-day and spiritual guidance.

Ginghamsburg is located in Tipp City, Ohio, a primarily white and middle-class community with a median household income that runs about 15 percent higher than the state average. Tipp City does have some residents who live at or below poverty level, but on the whole it is not particularly ethnically or socioeconomically diverse. Yet I have always considered it essential that the church reflect the full diversity of God's kingdom. A constant focus and challenge for my ministry has been to attract an economically and racially diverse congregation to our largely blue- and white-collar Tipp City campus.

Our two urban restart campuses, The Point in Trotwood and Fort McKinley in Dayton, have brought us closer to a Kingdom vision of what it means to embrace and model God's diversity. The Trotwood community is two-thirds African American and has its share of economic challenges. Fort McKinley averages a per capita income of only $18,000.

In both communities, especially Fort McKinley, ministry with the poor has become the core of what we do and a deep privilege. Rusty Eshleman, our worship and missions pastor for the campus, along with his wife Renae, insisted on moving into the community from the moment Rusty joined the Fort McKinley campus staff. They and their two preschool-age children work, play, eat, sleep, and share neighborhood crime watch duty with neighbors who by no means grew up in the same comfortable middle-class and rural contexts as the Eshlemans. Rusty insists that even if Ginghamsburg stopped paying him tomorrow, he wouldn't move out: "We feel called to the Fort McKinley neighborhood."

The Eshlemans understand that God is good, and God is just. If the gospel isn't good news for and with the poor, it isn't the gospel.

TIME AND MONEY

Before his Holy Club years at Oxford, one of the books that John Wesley named as most formative of his faith was

The Rules and Exercises for Holy Living and Dying by Jeremy Taylor. When I was in England last summer, I purchased a copy that was published in 1857. I had only read two pages before I began to see why Wesley admired it. Taylor writes, "No man is a better merchant than he who lays his time upon God and his money upon the poor."[14]

Money may seem limited, but time is even more limited. My entire life, your entire life, will be represented by a short dash engraved between two dates on a tombstone or memorial plaque. Both our time and our material resources are precious gifts from the hands of God. We and our churches will be held accountable on the final exam for having "proclaimed good news to the poor" and for investing our time and money wisely in those for whom God has declared, and repeatedly demonstrated, a special partiality.

A Few Ideas for Getting Started

- If you spot a need in your community and think, "Somebody should do something about this!" replace somebody with your own name. Make a commitment to be that servant. Recently my friend Rev. Pat Murray of Living Word Church in Vandalia, Ohio, led a morning devotion at our weekly staff chapel. As Pat taught from the parable of the good Samaritan, he simply looked up at one point and said, "If you come upon a need, you have found your ministry."

- Not sure what the greatest needs are among the poor in your community? Talk to your city, county, parish, or township officials. You will likely hear an earful. Find out how to partner with government, local school, or agency resources in that area of need.

- If you feel that you are too small or insignificant on your own to make a difference, see where God is already working through other churches, nonprofits, or agencies, and offer your services to help them.

- Find out which elementary school in your area has the greatest number of students on free or reduced-price breakfast or lunch programs. These schools may provide golden opportunities for mentoring, tutoring, and inviting children to develop new life pictures that may help them break the poverty cycle.

- Make sandwiches, and invite those whom you serve to join you in making them the next time around. Start your own Bologna Brigade.

- We serve a creative God who gave us our own creative God-spark. What passion burns in your heart? Act on it.

3
Creating New and Renewed Congregations

Jesus! the name that charms our fears, that bids our
sorrows cease; 'tis music in the sinner's ears, 'tis life,
and health, and peace.
Charles Wesley, "O For a Thousand Tongues to Sing"

LITTLE COUNTRY CHURCH

Next to the little country chapel that was the only Ginghamsburg "Church" I found when arriving in 1979, there's a somewhat dilapidated white house that used to serve as the parsonage. The structure was already past its prime thirty-six

73

years ago and hasn't improved with age. However, Ginghamsburg Boy Scout Troop #413 (as in Philippians 4:13) claims the house as its own and simply loves the old place.

Cleaning out the attic some months ago, a troop leader found and moved boxes of stored papers to our current main building for sorting and tossing. In the process, our staff uncovered a handwritten paper document with faded blue ink circa 1947 titled "Historical Sketch of Ginghamsburg U.B. Church." It detailed early church history including how the original grounds, where the chapel still stands, were donated by Rev. William L. Pence, a Baptist minister, with the stipulation that they were to be used for a union meeting house. The document states that until 1863 "Baptists, Dunkards, Campbellites, Lutherans, Methodists and United Brethren worshiped there." I love that heritage!

All that changed when circuit writer and evangelist B. W. Day, in charge of what was called the "Miami Circuit," was holding a "big meeting" in Vandalia, a few miles down the road from Ginghamsburg. As described in the document, Day "remarked to Bro. John Wells, 'As soon as I close my meeting in Vandalia, I will hold one in the Union Meeting House in Ginghamsburg.'" The story continues, "He held a six-week revival, and twenty souls were converted and fourteen of these formed a class which became the charter members of our present church." The report goes on to say that the first salary paid by the church was in 1864, when the grand sum of $14 was reported to the Quarterly Conference. The rest, as they say, is history.

That same restless Spirit that drove B. W. Day after an intensive revival in Vandalia to do it all over again just a few miles up the road in Ginghamsburg echoes the relentless thirst that early Methodists seem to have had in planting churches across America's countryside. This driving impulse to witness "to the ends of the earth"—and Ginghamsburg would have seemed like one of those "ends" back in 1863—was initiated by none other than Jesus Christ himself: "You will be my witnesses in Jerusalem, and in all Judea and Samaria, and to the ends of the earth" (Acts 1:8).

CALLED-OUT ONES

So, what happened to that driving impulse? When did Jesus' pioneers become Christian settlers, enclosed in our four walls, comfortable, and complacent? As noted in the introduction, the Towers Watson analysis classified more than one-third of our 32,228 United Methodist churches as dying or dead. When did we stop pouring "new wine into new wineskins" (Matthew 9:17)?

I suspect part of it happened when we downsized our definition of "church" to a children's nursery rhyme and finger play:

> This is the church
> This is the steeple
> Open it up
> And see all the people

A Greek word used throughout the New Testament for "church" is *ekklesia*, translated as "the called-out ones." Or, to quote the Apostle Peter, the church is "a chosen people, a royal priesthood, a holy nation, God's special possession, that you may declare the praises of him who called you out of darkness into his wonderful light" (1 Peter 2:9). The church of Jesus in the Book of Acts and Paul's epistles is never a building, much less a steeple.

I don't believe we are called by any means to do away with physical facilities that allow folks to gather for corporate worship and community, but I do believe we have defined church far too narrowly. While many of us are struggling to pay the mortgage and maintain the brick of our physical campuses, spiritual entrepreneurs have started thriving churches in homes, storefronts, movie theaters, microbreweries, and bars. Sounds to me like the places a twenty-first-century Jesus might like to hang out and connect with the least, the struggling, and the lost.

Jesus was an itinerant preacher, traveling across Judea, Galilee, and northern Israel. Although we often find him speaking in the synagogue when he walked into a new town, his ministry was certainly not limited to religious buildings. Homes, both those of friends and sometimes even of foes, often served as his "pulpit." In Luke 10:38-42, we see him teaching in the home of Lazarus, Mary, and Martha, with Mary at his feet listening avidly. In Luke 14:1, "when Jesus went to eat in the house of a prominent Pharisee, he was being carefully watched." I like to imagine Jesus helping himself to a generous second round of mashed potatoes while he schooled the pharisaic crowd about the sabbath and kingdom of God priorities.

Jesus taught from a boat in Matthew 13:2-3, and responded to questions in a field in Matthew 12:1-8. Scripture also describes Jesus teaching under trees, along the shore, by a well, and on mountainsides. His most famous sermon of all, the Sermon on the Mount, is historically assumed to have been delivered on the hillside of Mt. Eremos along the shore of the Sea of Galilee.

Similarly, the Apostle Paul did not allow any grass to grow under his feet as he helped to build the early church. The names of his epistles alone—Rome, Galatia, Ephesus, Philippi, Corinth— reveal that he was never tied to just one spot. Paul taught in a synagogue, by a riverside, in prison, in a marketplace, on a hilltop, in a formal academy, in a courtroom, in a council chamber, and on board a ship, just to name a few.

As evangelists, both Jesus and Paul spent more time seeking new faces in new places than they did preaching to an already-established choir from a familiar and comfortably well-worn pulpit. The message and the mission, were just too critical.

Although the Christian church was not founded until the New Testament era, the Old Testament has examples of God working through prophets and ordinary people to reach or embrace new groups. Joseph in a sense became an evangelist to the Egyptians as he demonstrated a lifestyle of wisdom and integrity, rising from the status of slave and prisoner to second in power only to Pharaoh.

In the Book of Esther we read how Esther and her uncle Mordecai served as God's agents of change in Persia. Likewise, Daniel, Meshach, Shadrach, and Abednego, through their lives and undiluted devotion to the one true God regardless of consequences, served as witnesses to the Babylonians. The King of Babylon, Nebuchadnezzar, was a polytheist who worshiped the gods Nabu and Marduk. However, after being restored to his senses following seven years of insanity, a period that resulted in part from his refusal to listen to Daniel, Nebuchadnezzar declared:

> "It is my pleasure to tell you about the miraculous signs and wonders that the Most High God has performed for me.
>
> How great are his signs,
>   how mighty his wonders!
> His kingdom is an eternal kingdom;
>   his dominion endures from generation to generation."
>   (Daniel 4:2-3)

A leader with a compelling call to spread the gospel is a powerful force. Influential evangelists through the years that have multiplied the Kingdom range from St. Patrick, Martin Luther, Jonathan Edwards, Charles Spurgeon, and George Whitefield to John and Charles Wesley, and even more recently to Billy Graham.

A GATEWAY OF HOPE

When they arrived in Portland, Maine, in 2007, Revs. Sara and Allen Ewing-Merrill shared two assignments: help a "remnant congregation" of a dozen retirees who had sold their large, historic church building determine their future and start a new church.

So they shared worship with the remnant of Chestnut Street United Methodist Church on Sunday mornings while they started New Light Community in their own dining room with weeknight dinners, prayer, conversation and service projects.

The clergy couple thought Chestnut Street would be a "hospice" situation—that they would care for that church until it decided to close. They soon learned otherwise.

"They really had this passion that God was finished with that building, but God wasn't finished with them, and that there was need for a strong United Methodist witness in downtown Portland," Allen said.

The Chestnut Street remnant bought a storefront space in downtown Portland, and when it opened in the spring of 2009, they shared it with New Light. The space helped both congregations connect with new people—and with each other. After about three years, the two faith communities merged to form HopeGateWay.

"It just kind of happened organically and naturally," Allen said.

HopeGateWay now has about one hundred worship attendees each Sunday, and a diverse group of about three hundred people connected there.

"We have the full socioeconomic spectrum, from [those who] slept outside last night, to retirees, to middle-class," Allen says.

Many HopeGateWay members participate in the recovery ministries that meet there.

"There's just not a strong line between our worshiping community and our recovery community. They really overlap," Allen said. "So we often preach about recovery concepts. It's not uncommon to talk about the 12 Steps in our sermons.... It goes way beyond not drinking to actually being well and whole and spiritually alive."

HopeGateWay also includes asylum seekers from Central Africa; in fact, the church started a nonprofit, Hope Acts, to better partner with those adjusting to life in the United States.

While worship at HopeGateWay couldn't be described as "traditional," it doesn't fit typical expectations behind the word "contemporary" either. Rather than a band or choir, the music is driven by a jazz pianist.

"If we do traditional hymns, we sort of liven them up," Sara says. "We also don't do praise and worship music; we do contemporary hymns" by composers such as Mark Miller and Shirley Erena Murray, as well as songs with non-English lyrics.

"Pretty much every week, we sing something in an African language—might be Kirundi, might be Swahili, which is a language that some of our folks speak—so when we do that, they're in the lead," Allen says. "It's really become kind of a signature thing that we sing global music."

Worship is interactive; questions posed during the sermon aren't rhetorical. "We actually expect people to talk about it," Allen says.

The active nature of HopeGateWay tends to attract those who might not otherwise find church relevant for their lives.

"I think that most of our people...wouldn't feel like they needed to go to church if they didn't have a community like HopeGateWay," Sara said. "They're not willing to just go to worship."

"It's because they see how people are living out their faith and really making a difference in the community," Allen said. "That is compelling to them."

JOHN WESLEY AND THE
OPEN-AIR GOSPEL

John Wesley was keenly thirsty to spread the gospel. Records indicate that during this lifetime he must have ridden at least 250,000 miles on horseback, or the equivalent of ten times around the middle of the earth. He is believed to have delivered more than forty thousand sermons, sometimes preaching up to three or more times per day. When the Anglican Church started closing its pulpits to him, Wesley would preach in the open air.

The first time he preached literally "in the field" was April 2, 1739. The day before, he had listened to George Whitefield, fellow evangelist and member of the Holy Club in Oxford, preach outdoors in Bristol, England. Prior to that day Wesley had been dubious about the appropriateness or efficacy of the open-air approach. However, following Whitefield's example, he gave it a go and began preaching in the venue that would become his hallmark in decades to come. Wesley noted, "At four in the afternoon I submitted to be more vile and proclaimed in the highways the glad tidings of salvation, speaking from a little eminence in a ground adjoining the city, to about three thousand people."[1] Wesley was hooked. He had realized his call just as Joseph, Esther, Daniel, Jesus, and the Apostle Paul had done in the centuries preceding.

Indeed, the people John Wesley spoke to in the open air might have seemed like barbarians to him. In *The Burning Heart*, author Skevington Wood notes, "Wesley was a dapper little man" who was "finical about his personal appearance" and "could not bear the slightest speck of dust on his clerical attire." Wood found it ironic that this same John Wesley would "expose himself to the four winds" and not "shrink back from the uncouth mob, which always surrounded him with filth and foul odours and often with heckling and violence." Funny the inconvenient things we will do for Jesus when we are committed to the way of the cross![2]

When skeptics questioned Wesley about the pace or expanse of his ministry, he would model his response after 1 Corinthians 9:16-17 and say, "I must go on; for a dispensation of the gospel is committed to me; and woe is me if I preach not the gospel."[3]

In addition to his open-air ministry, by the time John Wesley died in 1791 he had established 114 circuits encompassing 470 Methodist societies in Britain and Ireland. These circuits, representing seventy-two thousand Methodists, were served by three hundred full-time itinerant pastors and about two thousand lay preachers. By then, the Methodist movement had already started in the United States as well, with roughly sixty thousand Methodists in the newly independent country.

When Wesley died, one in thirty English adults was Methodist. In 1776, when the Declaration of Independence was signed, the US population was less than 2 percent Methodist. By 1850, it was 34 percent. What a contrast from the current decline of the mainline church![4]

MULTIPLICATION, NOT EXPANSION

As missiologist Alan Hirsh notes in his excellent book *The Forgotten Ways*, historically the church has experienced some astounding periods of church growth, or more specifically Christian growth. An approximate total of twenty-five thousand Christians in A.D. 100 had expanded to twenty million by A.D. 310. Hirsch also reminds us that the Christians of the day primarily operated illegally, with few Scriptures, no professional pastors, and no projectors or hazers in worship.[5]

China had a similar period of explosive Christian growth. When Mao Tse-tung began to purge religion from Chinese culture, there were two million Christians. Missionaries were banished and church property seized. Leaders were imprisoned; torture of Christians was not only legal but embraced. Yet, when missionaries were allowed back into China in the 1980s, they found sixty million Christians—thirty times as many as before Mao. How could this be?[6] If we could figure it out, maybe we could do it again! Clearly comfortable facilities, the best technology, and a supportive government ideology are not critical keys.

Ginghamsburg, in terms of worship attendance, is the fifth-largest church in the United Methodist denomination, and we have been known to use hazers now and again. Obviously the congregation didn't start out that way. God has had a unique anointing on this still-rural church surrounded by soybean fields on the outskirts of Tipp City, Ohio. When folks ask me how I managed to grow Ginghamsburg into a megachurch, I can only respond, "I didn't. God did."

Being a big church certainly has its advantages. We have a large pool of human capital to deploy into the world as the hands, feet, and voice of Jesus. Like other big churches, we have a larger pool of financial resources with which to do all the good we can, and by all the means we can. More than 60 percent of the money, goods, and other resources brought into Ginghamsburg is deployed back out for missional investment, so our operating budget runs a bit thin. Four weeks of cash in the bank, and sometimes less, is considered a win by our leadership board. I like to say we aren't rich, just blessed.

I am privileged to have been a part of the Ginghamsburg faith community for the past thirty-seven years. I am amazed and humbled by what God has accomplished. I am also increasingly convinced as the years go by that the megachurch is not the best answer for growing the Kingdom. The goal for most of us should not be to become the biggest church in the area, but to "church" the area—to multiply the church, not to expand it. After all, expanding ministry in just one place is a difficult feat in a world where gasoline is expensive, people can worship online, and younger generations want to feel part of authentic community.

As the folks at Ginghamsburg have come to realize, a better approach is to start a number of smaller churches. Besides creating churches that are tailored to the needs of the area, this approach enables us to model the ethnic and socioeconomic diversity that will be more reflective of the future Kingdom. As noted in the previous section, our restart of two failing churches in urban Dayton and Trotwood has gotten us closer to that more accurate picture of the kingdom of God.

Ginghamsburg merged with Fort McKinley in 2008 and launched The Point restart in 2012. The Fort is now a diverse, vibrant worshiping community of over 400 that has impacted, and is continuing to transform, its struggling Fort McKinley neighborhood in significant ways. The Point now worships approximately 120 folks weekly and has developed strong working partnerships with the city of Trotwood and the colocated YMCA branch for meaningful community impact. Both campuses are growing. We have no regrets about taking on either restart. However, not surprisingly, we have also validated along the way that taking on bricks and mortar and fairly significant initial staffing costs may not be a sustainable model. Future multiplication will require new models.

NEW MODELS OF MULTIPLICATION

This need for a different model is specifically why we were fortunate to add Rosario Picardo to our staff team in 2014.

Previously Roz had become the pastor of a "parachute drop" church for the United Methodist Kentucky Conference in 2008, when he moved into a challenging urban neighborhood to start a church in Lexington. He had no paid staff, no facility, and minimal start-up funding. Yet by the time he moved to Ohio in June 2014, his church start, Embrace, had grown into a multisite movement with diverse worshiping communities across three campuses. When he left, five pastors besides Rosario were serving the community. All but one were bi-vocational; three were unpaid, raising their own support and compensation as necessary for being part of the mission. Now, that is a sustainable model.[7]

I am convinced that the bi-vocational model will be key to most future worshiping communities. Scripture certainly provides bi-vocational examples. The prophet Amos earned his keep as a herdsmen and a fig farmer. Some of Jesus' early disciples were known to revert back to fishing now and again. Perhaps the most famous example is the Apostle Paul, who throughout his writings refers to his "day job" of being a tentmaker.

We first find out about Paul's trade in Acts 18:1-3:

> Paul left Athens and went to Corinth. There he met a Jew named Aquila, a native of Pontus, who had recently come from Italy with his wife Priscilla, because Claudius had ordered all Jews to leave Rome. Paul went to see them, and because he was a tentmaker as they were, he stayed and worked with them.

Paul indicates in multiple scriptures, including 1 Thessalonians 2:9, that he continued to ply his trade: "Surely you remember, brothers and sisters, our toil and hardship; we worked night and day in order not to be a burden to anyone while we preached the gospel of God to you."

Paul did not see a day trade as mutually exclusive of preaching the gospel; he seamlessly incorporated both into his life, at least when he wasn't imprisoned or shipwrecked. He reminded the elders of Ephesus,

"I have not coveted anyone's silver or gold or clothing. You yourselves know that these hands of mine have supplied my own needs and the needs of my companions. In everything I did, I showed you that by this kind of hard work we must help the weak, remembering the words the Lord Jesus himself said: 'It is more blessed to give than to receive.'"

(Acts 20:33-35)

In some sense, Paul's skilled trade also opened evangelism opportunities that otherwise may not have presented themselves. As he provided a needed skill in various communities, he would have had "teachable moments" with merchants, travelers, and customers. The trade would have provided him with additional credibility within a community and marketplace.

Although I am an ordained elder, highly valuing my seminary education and firmly believing there is a continuing place for credentialed elders within The United Methodist Church, I also recognize that Jesus did not change the world by creating a professional class of clergy; instead, he recruited and deployed hardworking laborers who had caught a Kingdom vision.

Rosario and the team are currently dreaming a new launch for Ginghamsburg in 2016. The next campus may be in either downtown Dayton or Huber Heights, a growing Dayton suburb that struggles a bit with community identity. Historically, Huber Heights has been known as "America's largest community of all brick homes." Now, there is nothing wrong with brick houses by any means, but by itself that is not a very compelling identity.

Making a Place
Inviting to New People

"This congregation went from a sleepy facility that people drove by to a parking lot that seems to be full all the time," said Rev. Duane Anders.

The senior pastor at Cathedral of the Rockies, the United Methodist Church in downtown Boise, Idaho, is speaking of the church's second campus. Amity United Methodist Church in the Boise Valley had an average attendance of about 70 when it voted to merge with Cathedral of the Rockies. Now, the Amity campus holds two services with a combined attendance of 240.

Anders had experience with multicampus churches, so he knew what questions to ask at the outset.

"I needed to know from the district superintendent that this was truly a merger: that both churches are in financially, in at every level," he said. "I also needed to know if Steve would come out of retirement."

"Steve" referred to Rev. Steve Tollefson, Anders's predecessor at Cathedral of the Rockies and the founding pastor of Amity. The merger would go more smoothly with support from someone both congregations trusted. "Steve agreed to come preach at Amity for a year," Anders said. "It gave the two campuses a connection from the start."

While some mergers begin with a complete shutdown of the smaller campus, that didn't happen with Amity.

"It was more of a natural progression," Anders said. "Probably the biggest shift that happened was we rallied the troops and asked who would commit to spending a year at the Amity campus. We said, 'This is your chance to be a missionary in your own backyard, and you're still part of the Cathedral. Not just to go there to fill the seats, but to go there and know you're a servant.'"

From the outside, Heaton Chapel is the most obvious change. When a member of the Cathedral campus offered funding for a new building at the Amity campus—on the condition that they build immediately—Anders and other leaders prayed about whether it was the right thing to do. And it seems that it was.

"Heaton Chapel opened the door for a level of growth that we probably couldn't currently be at as quickly," he said. "It created a whole new level of buzz. We also took down a fence that had wound up being a barrier to the community. Folks from the neighborhood have engaged."

One way Amity extends welcome is through weekly food truck nights. "We open the fellowship area and do hospitality for people who stay to eat," Anders said. "It took a couple of months for people to go, 'Oh, anybody can come? This isn't just for church people?' I've since met active families who first came to the church because of the food trucks.

"I think any time you merge, the risk is about, 'Who are we? Where did our identity go?' But people are learning a new identity at both campuses. We are viewing each worship service as a congregation, so we have six congregations, two sites, one church. People's perspectives have changed a lot."

However, Huber Heights recently added a popular outdoor music and entertainment amphitheater that is creating a buzz. The city is considering a development proposal for a mixed-use area on sixty-seven acres near the amphitheater that could feature retail, hospitality, restaurants, and office space.[8] Downtown Dayton is experiencing a revitalization of sorts, with more young professionals in particular moving in. Both of these areas feel ripe for the gospel of Jesus Christ.

Although it is too soon to know the location or venue for this next church start, we do know that it will not be a heavily staffed brick-and-mortar church operation. In downtown Dayton, potential locations include an alternative movie theater near the city's historic Oregon district or a popular craft beer brewery. A Huber Heights church plant would also co-share an existing facility, whether it be a movie theater, eatery, or some other public-oriented venue. The campus pastor will be bi-vocational and unlikely to be ordained. In addition to a pastor, initial staff will probably include a worship leader and children's minister, either initially unpaid, on a limited contract, or bi-vocational with primary income through a different source.

I highly appreciate the paid staff of Ginghamsburg Church. Our mission and ministry rely in many ways on their leadership. Once my daughter-in-law asked me how I managed to get so much done. My response was, "How did Moses part the Red Sea?" The answer, of course, is with his staff. Yet I also remind myself and the staff periodically that we are mercenaries for the Kingdom, paid for what others do willingly for free. Like the growing church in the fourth century, I think the next movement requires more unpaid servant recruits who are sold out to the mission of Jesus, and fewer paid professional servants. This conclusion is based on economic reality, as well as on the historical evidence of what leads to success in times of rapidly growing Christian movements.

IN COMMUNITY

At Ginghamsburg's largest campus in Tipp City, we offer five worship celebrations each weekend—two on Saturday and three on Sunday. We can accommodate about four thousand worshipers with that schedule on any given weekend—not that the experience isn't somewhat of a marathon for the weekend's preacher and other staff required to support that many worship celebrations.

That's a lot of worshipers, but think how many more we could accommodate with multiple churches. If eventually we are able to birth one hundred vibrant and incarnational churches across the Miami Valley, the region where we are located that encompasses roughly eight Ohio counties, and each church had one hundred worshipers per week, we would have ten thousand additional worshipers, or a church of fourteen thousand. Smaller venues, besides welcoming more people, can meet the felt needs of the indigenous neighborhoods, make more room for Jesus' followers to deploy their gifts and talents, and multiply Kingdom reach and impact. This is about "churching the area," not being the biggest "church in the area."

In our smaller campuses at Fort McKinley and The Point, a sense of community seems to happen naturally. At our Tipp City campus, which pulls people from a multicounty area, we have to work harder at it. Again recognizing that things are better in circles than in rows, we make a special effort to help folks connect with the community through life groups.

Of course, each campus has its own unique qualities. When I am not scheduled to preach or travel, one of my favorite ways to experience Sunday morning is by doing "progressive worship." Carolyn and I start out at 8:30 with Soul Food Café at the Fort. We enjoy a hot, delicious breakfast while worshiping in the Fort's sunny community room with a number of nontraditional worshipers that include homeless folks, recovering addicts, and a host of diverse Fort neighbors. There is an electric buzz in the air from the moment we enter the building, along with the inviting smells of food on the griddle.

Next we move to The Point, located in a shopping center in the space we share with the YMCA, for 10:00 worship. The first room we enter is basically a restaurant-style area with pancakes and prayer served up before worship. When I hear the music starting in the worship center, just beyond the breakfast area, it's hard to make myself go in, because it feels like worship is already happening over breakfast.

We then drive north to participate in 11:30 worship at Tipp City, always an excellent and powerful experience. At the same time, Tipp City lacks the space and organic opportunity for community as folks walk in the door. There is a sense of welcome and relationship in a smaller venue that has to be intentionally created and fostered in a megachurch lobby—not impossible by any means but more difficult.

Acts 2 makes it clear that community among believers was a key to growth in the early church. Strong community— "we are all in this together"—created a movement that could not only survive but thrive amidst adversity and persecution. There is no such thing as a magic formula for multiplying a movement, but if there were, it might read a lot like Acts 2:42-47.

> They devoted themselves to the apostles' teaching and to
> fellowship, to the breaking of bread and to prayer. Everyone
> was filled with awe at the many wonders and signs performed

by the apostles. All the believers were together and had everything in common. They sold property and possessions to give to anyone who had need. Every day they continued to meet together in the temple courts. They broke bread in their homes and ate together with glad and sincere hearts, praising God and enjoying the favor of all the people. And the Lord added to their number daily those who were being saved.

Let's look at the key components described in that passage. A church multiplies when:

- The church realizes it cannot do it alone. Constant exposure to teaching and the practice of prayer reinforces our dependence on God.
- Community is a necessity, not a luxury. All believers "were together" and devoted to the "breaking of bread."
- An abundance mentality means that all needs can and will be provided for when the gifts and resources of the community are combined.
- The poor are included; their needs are met.
- Praise is constant for what has already been provided; an attitude of gratitude is the status quo.
- The community that's demonstrated in the church serves as a model or witness to the larger world, "enjoying the favor of all people."
- God does the hard work, and we give God the praise for it.

I have to admit, those seven verses pack a bigger punch and deliver more truth about new and renewed congregations than the rest of my chapter combined.

THE THREE R'S

One of my heroes is Dr. John Perkins, a pastor, civil rights activist, and community developer. John knows what it means to put your life on the line for what you believe. In 1970, he was arrested and beaten by police after leading an economic boycott of white-owned stores in Mendenhall, Mississippi. Instead of allowing this and other difficult experiences to sour him, John developed a commitment to holistic ministry, believing that racism inflicts bondage on all people, those who propagate it and those who are its victims. He started a number of ministries that have focused on the gospel as well as on community needs, and, along with his wife, he founded the John and Vera Mae Perkins Foundation in Jackson, Mississippi. Ginghamsburg mission teams were blessed with the opportunity to partner with Dr. Perkins in constructing a guesthouse for the foundation in the late 1990s.

John also founded the Christian Community Development Association (CCDA) in 1989, a network of church congregations and other nonprofits that work in economically struggling urban areas. The mission of the CCDA is "to inspire, train, and connect Christians who seek to bear witness to the Kingdom of God by reclaiming and restoring under-resourced communities." The organization summarizes its philosophies with three R's: relocation, reconciliation, and redistribution. Let's take a minute to look at these and think about how they relate to churches.[9]

Relocation

I love John 1:14 as translated in The Message. It proclaims, "The Word became flesh and blood, and moved into the neighborhood." That verse is the perfect illustration of what relocation is all about. The CCDA believes in incarnational ministry, just the way Jesus did it. It claims, "By relocating, a person will understand most clearly the real problems facing the poor; and then he or she may begin to look for real solutions."[10] Let's extrapolate this to church planting. It's hard to reach a community where, as a church, you are unwilling to live. We not only need to plant in the places where we are called to reach others for Christ; at least some of us need to live there too. We can't just be commuters from the burbs.

Reconciliation

In the CCDA lexicon, reconciliation is both of people with God and of people with each other. Clearly our churches are to be about the former, but sometimes we ignore the latter. I agree with John Perkins that we need to be intentional about bringing "people of all races and cultures into the one worshiping body of Christ"—another great argument for creating new spaces in perhaps unexpected places. How do we intentionally go about growing faith communities that fully reflect the diversity and richness of God's kingdom?[11]

Redistribution

We serve a God with cattle on a thousand hills (Psalm 50:10), as I mentioned earlier, and there are resources enough for all. Redistribution is about an abundance mentality rather than a scarcity mentality. As the CCDA points out, bringing our skills and resources as a church into new neighborhoods adds to the resource pool of the entire community. Collectively all can be well served.[12] This reflects back to ministry *with* the poor, not *to* the poor. A rising tide lifts all boats, as the saying goes.

The CCDA philosophy has been influential in Pastor Rosario Picardo's ministry. When Roz married his wife, Callie, he moved into a home that Callie already owned in a nice Lexington suburb.

PARTICIPATE IN OUR DREAM
(MALAWI)

The true Methodist philosophy of a holistic ministry is alive in the Malawi Provisional Annual Conference, as the conference experiences the real impact and transformation of communities to the glory of God wherever a Methodist community of faith is planted. Through important ministries such as health initiatives, poverty programs, and leadership development, we participate in what God is doing in the world, and we dream of becoming a self-sustaining African Annual Conference by 2020.

One of our ministries is the Nutrition Clinics at Nancholi in Blantyre and at Madisi in Dowa District. Persons living with HIV/AIDS come to the clinics, some with weights as low as sixty pounds; they gain weight to as much as ninety pounds after receiving food supplements. A client in Madisi, Mr. Kadiwa, had this to say: "The Nutrition Clinic has become the basis of my still being alive today. I should have been dead were it not for this small house of hope."

Also in the field of health, the Mwachedwa Village T/A Mbenje in Nsanje District has seen net distribution carried out in the community, drastically reducing the malaria occurrence recorded at Sorgin Health Clinic. We praise God for protecting our communities from the deadly malaria disease, and thanks be to the United Methodist Committee on Relief (UMCOR), which has supported the program and enabled United Methodists to make a great witness in the area as well.

As a Provisional Annual Conference, we have programs of poverty alleviation. The micro-finance program, supported by resolution of the General Conference in 2012, has seen more success as groups gain access to loans and families are able to send their children to school because living costs are now met. This success spills over to our members who have started to support church programs in a way they did not do previously.

We have a farm in Mchinji as part of the sustainability plan for the conference budget operations. We are working on diversified agriculture, growing bananas, rearing pigs, and planting seeds to maximize productivity and profits. This has given us hope.

In the area of leadership, we have made great strides in that we have started to harvest graduates in our church from institutions such as Africa University in Zimbabwe, and these graduates are filling key roles in the running of the conference. Helping to coordinate the leadership program is Rev. Klaus Schmiegel, a missionary from Germany. The graduates include both clergy and laity, which has given us real hope.

Our dream and desire is to become a self-sustaining African Annual Conference. We ask that you participate in our dream and share what God is doing in our very times.

—*Daniel Mhone*

However, Roz felt a disconnect every time he drove in from his comfortable community to the urban campuses of Embrace. That drive took his time, took his gas, and took him away from an incarnational "all-in" presence in the campus neighborhoods. He and Callie decided to sell the more expensive home and purchase a smaller property, priced at half the cost of their first home. The new homestead was located between their two urban campuses. Rosario as pastor immediately became more accessible, and in a sense more legitimate, to those who called Embrace home, as well as to those Embrace was working to reach.

When the Picardos followed God's call to Ginghamsburg for Roz to pursue new church development and serve as campus pastor at The Point, he and Callie bought a home in Trotwood, The Point's community, for a third of what they paid for their most recent home in Lexington.

The Picardos shop at Trotwood businesses as much as possible and work out at the Trotwood YMCA. When they first arrived, Roz spent hours each month at the local barbershop, a hub of community connection, although he has no hair to speak of. Now the Picardos are beginning to look for housing opportunities in downtown Dayton, as Ginghamsburg prepares to plant there.

Rosario and Callie model the three R's of relocation, reconciliation, and redistribution and are committed to making the church incarnational with its neighbors.

MULTIPLICATION IN ONE PLACE

Now that we've looked at growing vital churches in new places, let's talk about creating a vital church in the same space. This can be done, at least initially, by offering worship at additional times. The first church "multiplication" at Ginghamsburg happened when we added additional Sunday morning worship times, eventually moving to Saturday evenings as well. New times make it possible for more people to join the community. Worshiping on Saturday evening may seem like a difficult sacrifice, but for many it's the only time that works. I got the idea when driving by Tipp City's Catholic church on a Saturday night and seeing the parking lot filled for mass. We tried it at our church, and now we have five to six hundred people in worship each Saturday night who might not be at church otherwise. In Kingdom economics, one pastor working Saturday evening for hundreds of folks is a worthwhile investment.

One of our Saturday evening venues is smaller in terms of attendance but meets a specialized need. Next Step Recovery Celebration adds the nuances of 12-Step meetings to create a powerful time of worship. Next Step is one of my favorite times to preach each week because it draws people who don't need convincing about how much they really need Jesus.

Soul Food Café at Fort McKinley grew when it simply moved to a different space in the same church building. We had offered a free, hot breakfast to neighbors in the Fort's Community Room from the first Sunday after we merged with the original Fort McKinley Church. It was always a challenge to entice breakfast guests to head downstairs to the more traditional sanctuary for worship after breakfast. So we moved worship up to them. It worked! Sometimes "third places" can be found within a church's existing facilities.

Online worship is another way to expand ministry. Of course, it is also the most difficult for developing true community. The topic is too big for this book, but I do want to note that United Methodist Communications provides ideas for broadcasting worship for free at www.umcom.org. Another helpful resource is www .churchonlineplatform.com. Some churches, including our own campus at The Point, are using the increasingly popular social media app Periscope for live broadcasts of worship.

THE LEADERSHIP BARRIER

An excellent resource for planting new churches is Path 1, a focus of United Methodist Discipleship Ministries.[13] Path 1 offers planting, training, and coaching resources for churches. I recommend Path 1 as a starting point for you as you begin to dream of creating new places for new faces.

Whatever resources you seek out and use, I believe that ultimately the greatest barrier to growing vital churches is not financial. The barrier is leadership. Pastor Roz knows that he may be able to start a new campus initially, but it will only grow into a vital and sustainable faith movement if he identifies and coaches the right missional pastor to take over as Roz moves on. This is why, among the Four Areas of Focus, Creating New and Renewed Congregations is so closely related to Developing Principled Christian Leaders.

With this in mind, Roz is building a church planter residency program at Ginghamsburg, called Rooted. This two-year, full-time residency is a paid training/internship program for developing lay or clergy participants into church planters. Residents will work with Ginghamsburg and our campuses to receive hands-on experience in community outreach, evangelism, preaching, worship planning, building development, life group leadership, and financial stewardship. The goal of the residency program is to identify, develop, and deploy church planters who are gifted, called, and prepared to lead a launch team in starting a new church site that reflects Ginghamsburg's missional DNA. Our vision is to develop a network of one thousand churches by 2050, and to do so we need to take an active role in developing future generations of principled leaders who will plant and grow them.

THE GLOBAL WITNESS

Planting new faith communities may feel like a challenging proposition, and it is. Yet despite the decline of mainline denominations and churches in North America, church multiplication is exploding in other, far more challenging parts of the world.

One example I've witnessed firsthand is the United Methodist Church movement in Vietnam, a communist holdout country that has not yet legally authorized the existence of United Methodism. Thankfully, local officials in certain regions have taken a more favorable stance in allowing the church to operate publicly. Open Doors, an organization that serves persecuted Christians, ranks Vietnam sixteenth out of all nations on its World Watch List for Christian persecution.[14]

In spite of persecution, since pastors Ut and Karen Vo-To became missionaries to Vietnam in 2002, The United Methodist Church's Vietnam Mission Initiative has grown to include more than three hundred churches, with 270 pastors and fourteen local elders. A reported fifteen thousand people participate in Vietnamese-led house churches.[15]

A few years ago I was invited to train Vietnamese pastors for a week in Ho Chi Minh City. Although I knew it was potentially a risky undertaking for me personally in a place where the church was essentially illegal, my concern was more than offset when I witnessed the courage and commitment of the pastors who attended the training. They traveled in from across the Vietnamese countryside, showing passionate commitment to Jesus and to reaching the people of Vietnam. Compared to the risks they took, mine seemed minor. After all, following the training I would fly back to the United States and they would stay. It was their home, and they were determined to claim it for the Kingdom. Watching them eliminated any excuses I previously had had about church planting being hard, costly, or inconvenient.

Jesus told his disciples in Luke 10:2, "The harvest is plentiful, but the workers are few. Ask the Lord of the harvest, therefore, to send out workers into his harvest field." We are surrounded by a cloud of witnesses, waiting to see if we are willing to work God's prepared harvest. Christ has done the hard part. We just need to supply the "want to," the "work to," and the faith.

A Few Ideas for Getting Started

- Before trying a church plant in a new place, ask if you have maximized what can be accomplished to share the good news in your current space. Is there an unreached segment of your community that could be better served if you offered worship at a different time of day, on a new day of the week, or in a different space in your current facility? For instance, you could use your church's sanctuary, community room, or family life center to add a 12-step recovery worship on Saturday night, a difficult time of week for many who struggle with addiction. In other words, before reaching out, use what is already in your hands.

- Is there a setting where you already do ministry that could become a vital church community? For instance, if you have an effective care ministry in a nearby assisted living or long-term care facility, could that become a worshiping community or a video venue?

- As described in the chapter, explore beginning an online worship experience that does not require brick and mortar.

- Equip your sold-out Jesus followers to start their own small, informal communities. Is it possible that the group of folks meeting on Wednesday night in a nearby pub over beverages and the Bible could be transformed into a new faith community?

- Can college students who are away at school start a dorm-room church that watches the live stream of your worship together each week, along with supporting discipleship resources?
- Move into the neighborhood that you see as your church's next place of evangelistic calling—I mean, literally move in. Once you're in, hold an "open table" night each week and offer a standing invitation to your new neighbors to drop in to your home for dinner. You can provide the main dish if they want to bring something to share. This approach might drive the menu planners among us a little crazy, but look what Jesus was able to accomplish with fish and a few loaves of bread. Holding weekly dinners is a great way to create contagious feelings of community that can serve as rich soil for new church plants.

4
Improving Global Health

We weep for those that weep below, and burdened, for
the afflicted sigh; The various forms of human woe excite
our softest sympathy, Fill every heart with mournful care,
and draw out all our souls in prayer.
—Charles Wesley, "Let God, Who Comforts the Distressed"

THE GOD WHO HEALS

It's appropriate that our final area of focus within the passionate
church is abundant health. In essence, the work of the gospel is
to reconcile a broken world with its Creator, returning all of God's

earth and those who abide on it to full health. Principled Christian disciples must lead the charge, producing the fruit on others' trees that transforms lives. Many of the health crises that plague the world, especially in terms of physical health, can be directly linked to poverty and the resultant lack of access to nourishing food, safe water, lifesaving medications, and preventative health care. Also, vibrant, incarnational churches are crucial for healing and empowering entire communities. As Christians, we are called to work holistically within the world to bring God's kingdom to planet earth.

Abundant health is an emphasis throughout Scripture. In the Old Testament, we see God at times referred to as *Jehovah Rapha*, or the God who heals. One of the first examples occurs following the miraculous parting of the Red Sea that allowed God's people to escape the wrath of Pharaoh's army and prompted the people to sing God's praises in Exodus 15:1-21. However, by three verses and three days later, just a few miles up the road, the people were already grumbling about a lack of water. The Lord appeared to Moses, showing him how to "heal" the bitter waters of Marah where the people had stopped so that all might drink:

> There the Lord issued a ruling and instruction for them and put them to the test. He said, "If you listen carefully to the Lord your God and do what is right in his eyes, if you pay attention to his commands and keep all his decrees, I will not bring on you any of the diseases I brought on the Egyptians, for I am the Lord [Jehova Rapha], who heals you."
>
> (Exodus 15:25-26)

The Hebrew word *rapha*, meaning to heal, restore, or cure, appears in the Old Testament more than sixty times. We see it used again in the context of "healing" the water when, in 2 Kings, the people of Jericho complained to the prophet Elisha that the city's water was bad:

> Then he went out to the spring and threw the salt into it, saying, "This is what the Lord says: 'I have healed this water. Never again will it cause death or make the land unproductive.'" And the water has remained pure to this day, according to the word Elisha had spoken.
>
> (2 Kings 2:21-22)

Later in 2 Kings, Hezekiah, the king of Judah, was severely ill to the point of death. Although warned by the prophet Isaiah that he had better put his affairs in order because he was about to die, Hezekiah turned his face to the wall, urgently praying to the Lord, reminding God of his faithfulness and devotion. God heard, and then God healed, another example of *rapha*.

> Before Isaiah had left the middle court, the word of the Lord came to him: "Go back and tell Hezekiah, the ruler of my people, 'This is what the Lord, the God of your father David, says: I have heard your prayer and seen your tears; I will heal you. On the third day from now you will go up to the temple of the Lord. I will add fifteen years to your life.'"
>
> (2 Kings 20:4-6)

The book of Psalms repeatedly mentions and praises God as healer. Psalm 30:2 declares: "Lord my God, I called to you for help, and you healed me." We read in Psalm 41:3, "The Lord sustains them on their sickbed and restores them from their bed of illness." The psalmist proclaims in Psalm 147:3, "He heals the brokenhearted and binds up their wounds." Psalm 107:19-20 reassures us, "They cried to the Lord in their trouble, and he saved them from their distress. He sent out his word and healed them;

Connecting with Global Health Movement Revitalizes Small Church

A few years ago, Rupert United Methodist Church in the small town of Rupert, Vermont, was down to just eight regular attendees, many of whom were over age ninety.

"The church almost closed its doors," said Tom Atkins. "When our superintendent came to see us, he said, 'Yes, you can close the doors, or if you still want to worship here you can get supply pastors.'"

The congregation chose the latter option.

"They asked me if I would fill in when they couldn't get one of the retired Methodist pastors to do it," said Atkins, a member of Rupert UMC who had a seminary degree.

After a few months, he became their primary preacher. He eventually became licensed as a local pastor and was appointed part-time to the congregation. But long before that arrangement became official, Atkins realized that this congregation had become isolated from its United Methodist connections.

"I felt very strongly that part of what we needed to do was get reconnected with the denomination, and get reconnected with helping other people," he said. "And just about that time, we heard about Imagine No Malaria. What's beautiful about that program is that it gives you something that just an average member can take hold of: $10 saves a life. That's about as clear as you can get."

Members learned more about their denomination's part in the fight against malaria—a deadly disease that is treatable, curable, and preventable. They set out to see how many lives they could save, $10 at a time (the cost of an insecticide-treated bed net to ward off malaria-carrying mosquitoes). That first year, they raised $270—enough to save twenty-seven lives. To celebrate, Atkins designed a bulletin cover with twenty-seven faces on it, illustrating the impact.

"That really did something for them," he said. "They suddenly realized that little teeny Rupert Methodist Church could make a difference in people's lives in a way that they had forgotten they could do."

The following year, they raised $570.

"They started to tell their friends about it....This was them taking hold of something and making a difference," Atkins said. "Yes, we saved fifty-seven lives, but I really believe we also made a big difference in ourselves. They felt much more a part of a larger church."

And they are a larger church themselves: Rupert UMC now averages twenty-three people in worship per week, with another eight or ten regular visitors from New York who spend weekends in the area.

"What we did in the scope of Imagine No Malaria is tiny, tiny, tiny," Atkins says, but it spurred the church into action. Rupert UMC went from doing one charitable project per year to partnering with local social service agencies: They're beginning to renovate their long-vacant parsonage to fit the agencies' needs for a suitable space to meet with clients.

"I really think Imagine No Malaria was the catalyst to help them realize, 'Yes, we're a little church, but there are things we can do and there are differences we can make,'" Atkins says. "That moved them to think a little bigger and dream a little bigger and look for things where we really could make a difference."

he rescued them from the grave." (I recommend that you find a moment today and read all of Psalm 107; in a sense it could serve as an encompassing theme passage for *The Passionate Church*.)

HEALING IN HIS WINGS

Abundant health is also an emphasis in Scripture passages about Jesus. When foretelling the coming Messiah, Malachi prophesies, "But to you who fear My name the Sun of Righteousness shall arise with healing in His wings" (Malachi 4:2 NKJV). The metaphor evokes the image of a bird that gathers its chicks safely under its wings to heal them. The Hebrew word for "wings" in the passage is *kanaph*, which, as noted in Strong's Concordance, has multiple definitions in addition to wing, including "border," "extremity," or "corner of a garment."[1]

The Malachi 4:2 image evokes for me the miracle of Jesus healing the woman with the issue of blood in Matthew 9:20-22:

> Just then a woman who had been subject to bleeding for twelve years came up behind him and touched the edge of his cloak. She said to herself, "If I only touch his cloak, I will be healed." Jesus turned and saw her. "Take heart, daughter," he said, "your faith has healed you." And the woman was healed at that moment.

In our chapter on ministry with the poor, we noted that Jesus declared his mission statement as he quoted Isaiah in the front of Nazareth's synagogue.

> "The Spirit of the Lord is on me,
>   because he has anointed me
>   to proclaim good news to the poor.

> He has sent me to proclaim freedom for the prisoners
> > and recovery of sight for the blind,
> to set the oppressed free,
> > to proclaim the year of the Lord's favor."
> > > (Luke 4:18-19)

Jesus' mission was clearly restorative as he prepared to proclaim the good news and the year of the Lord's favor. Jesus' mission was also one of healing, providing "recovery of sight for the blind." Now, that healing should clearly be interpreted on the spiritual level, but the fruits of his ministry demonstrated Jesus' concern for physical healing as well. Per my count, Jesus performed at least twenty-six specifically documented healing miracles across the four Gospels and twenty-seven if you count his own resurrection, which you might call the ultimate form of healing. If you add up the multiple lepers, demoniacs, and blind folks healed miraculously at the same time, the number jumps to thirty-nine. Six of the people Jesus healed were literally blind.

Of course, we know from John 21:25 that Jesus performed even more miracles than the thirty-nine I've counted: "Jesus did many other things as well. If every one of them were written down, I suppose that even the whole world would not have room for the books that would be written."

Physical disabilities or ailments that Jesus healed included blindness, leprosy, deafness and muteness, fever, paralysis, dropsy, ear amputation, and a withered hand. We might call him an especially talented general practitioner who had a few unique specialties to boot. And his healing of lives was not simply physical. Depending on how we choose interpret it, Jesus also cured mental illness, emotional distress, or demonic possessions on at least three occasions. His most miraculous healings involved overcoming death: the widow's son in Luke 7, the religious leader's daughter in Matthew 9, his friend Lazarus in John 11, and his own in Luke 24.

Although it's thrilling to note these examples of Jesus' healings in the Bible, the rest of us are by no means off the hook. Jesus told his disciples in John 14:12, "Very truly I tell you, whoever believes in me will do the works I have been doing, and they will do even greater things than these, because I am going to the Father." We will return to our responsibility in a moment.

WESLEY AND HIS *PRIMITIVE PHYSICK*

John Wesley considered physical health and wholeness to be a matter of spiritual concern. In Wesley's ministry with the poor, he not only worked for spiritual healing but for physical care and restoration. His book, *Primitive Physick*, first published anonymously in 1747, was written to serve as practical medical information and advice for those who not afford a private physician's care.

In the book's preface, Wesley describes the importance of physical health and how we influence it by our eating and exercise choices. Wesley goes on in the preface to list what he viewed as rules for healthy living. The list is far too long to recount, but here are some great examples of advice that our medical community would espouse even today, nearly three hundred years later.

- "The great rule of eating and drinking is to suit the quality and quantity of food to the strength of the digestion; to take always such a sort and such a measure of food as sits light and easy on the stomach."
- "A due degree of exercise is indispensably necessary to health and long life."

- "Everyone that would preserve health should be as clean and sweet as possible in their houses, clothes, and furniture."
- "Those who read or write much, should learn to do it standing; otherwise, it will impair their health."[2]

That final piece of advice feels particularly prescient today. Over the past couple of years, the media have been full of reports about recent studies on the dangers of too much sitting, even if a person exercises regularly. A sedentary lifestyle increases the likelihood of heart disease, diabetes, and premature death.[3]

Of course, Wesley was not always accurate in his advice. One of his suggestions for curing a headache was to "apply to each temple the thin yellow rind of a lemon, newly pared off." I think I will stick with Tylenol®! The treatment for an obstructed bowel was to "hold a live puppy constantly on the belly." Once again, I love dogs, but...Nonetheless, we see that John Wesley was deeply concerned with wholeness in health, both physical and spiritual.[4]

Wesley wrote in a letter to friend and theologian Alexander Knox in 1778:

> But it will be a double blessing if you give yourself up to the Great Physician, that He may heal soul and body together. And unquestionably this is His design. He wants to give you and my dear Mrs. Knox both inward and outward health.[5]

Primitive Physick was not Wesley's only practical solution for meeting physical health needs. He opened clinics in Bristol and London as well as a dispensary where people could obtain medicine. Also in each local area with a Methodist presence, Wesley established the office of "visitor of the sick." This office would typically be filled by a woman who would call upon the ill in hopes of meeting physical and spiritual needs, often drawing on Wesley's book to help determine a course of action.[6]

WORLDWIDE PROGRESS

Based on the teachings of Scripture and reinforced by John Wesley, our responsibility as Christians is clear: we are held accountable for the ministries of health and healing. Jesus healed the sick and disabled; we are to serve the sick and disabled.

According the World Health Organization (WHO), we have made progress globally. In its 2014 list of Ten Facts on the State of Global Health, the first fact was encouraging: life expectancy at birth had increased by six years since 1990.

> A baby born in 2012 could expect to live to 70 years on average—62 years in low-income countries to 79 years in high-income countries. Life expectancy at birth is based on the death rates across all age groups in a population in a given year—children and adolescents, adults and the elderly.[7]

Most of the other facts were not as encouraging. If I were playing poker I would preface the list by saying, "Read 'em and weep."

- Around 6.6 million children under the age of 5 die each year.
- Preterm birth (born alive before 37 weeks of pregnancy) complications are the leading killer of newborn babies worldwide.
- Cardiovascular diseases are the leading causes of death in the world. Even more sadly, at least 80 percent of premature deaths from cardiovascular diseases could be prevented. More on this later.

- Though death from AIDS-related causes is steadily decreasing from a peak of 2.3 million deaths in 2005 to an estimated 1.6 million deaths in 2012, there is still global inequality in treatment, care, and education. In 2012 nearly 70 percent of HIV/AIDS deaths occurred in sub-Saharan Africa.
- Every day, about 800 women die due to complications of pregnancy and childbirth.
- Mental health disorders such as depression are among the 20 leading causes of disability across the world.
- Cigarette smoking may be on the decline in the United States, but that is not the case globally.[8] Tobacco kills nearly 6 million people each year. According to the WHO, 5 million or more of those deaths are from direct tobacco use, and more than 600,000 nonsmokers die from exposure to second-hand smoke. The WHO predicts the annual death toll could rise to more than eight million by 2030.
- Almost 1 in 10 adults has diabetes, with diabetes causing 1.5 million deaths in 2012.
- Nearly 3,500 people die from road traffic crashes every day. This statistic may technically be outside the scope of "global health," but someone reading this book may feel a God-nudge to work toward a Kingdom solution.[9]

As we can see from the list, the church has plenty of work to do as a healing presence of Christ in the world, and it's going to take more than *Primitive Physick* to tackle it. Of course, the church alone can't do it all. Tackling dangerous and systemic killer diseases takes partnership and cooperation among governments, health agencies, nongovernmental organizations (NGOs), medical researchers, and philanthropists.

We can't do it alone, but we can take heart from the fact that when the church commits to resolving a global health disaster, it does make a difference. Two primary examples would be in the battles against AIDS and malaria.

The AIDS Struggle

As shown in previous figures, deaths from AIDS are on the decline; however, AIDS still is not curable. There is work left to be done. But more effective treatments are now available and at more affordable costs. The rate of new infections also has dropped because of better education and safer sex and health practices.[10]

The United Nation's AIDS organization, UNAIDs, reported in July of 2014: "The global response to HIV has averted 30 million new HIV infections and 7.8 million AIDS-related deaths since 2000," adding that "had the world stood back to watch the epidemic unfold, the annual number of new HIV infections is likely to have risen to around 6 million by 2014." The report also noted, however, that the struggle isn't over. Per UNAIDS, 36.9 million people still are infected with the human immunodeficiency virus (HIV) that causes AIDS, and more than one million people die annually, many as already noted in sub-Saharan Africa. There's still no vaccine for prevention and no cure. Two million people are infected annually, and more than a million die of AIDS.[11]

Part of the good news can be attributed to efforts of the global church. The Catholic Church, somewhat controversially because of its stance against condom use, has been a key contributor in the fight against AIDS. Vatican statistics in 2012 revealed that Catholic Church-related organizations provide nearly 25 percent of "all HIV treatment, care, and support throughout the world and run more than 5000 hospitals, 18,000 dispensaries and 9,000 orphanages, many involved in AIDS-related activities." That level of support is significant. Without the Catholic Church, who else would have carried one-quarter of the load?[12]

The United Methodist denomination has also been actively serving on the AIDS front. Since the United Methodist Global AIDS Fund (UMGAF) was established at the 2004 General Conference, it has funded, in partnership with United Methodist Global Ministries, 287 HIV and AIDS projects in forty-four countries. Prevention, care, and treatment advocacy has also been a hallmark of the UMGAF focus. In addition, dozens of United Methodist annual conferences have undertaken AIDS-focused projects.[13]

IMAGINE NO MALARIA

Arguably the largest-scale and most successful United Methodist commitment to global health has been Imagine No Malaria (INM), the successor to an earlier grass-roots initiative called Nothing But Nets. Through INM, the United Methodist Church committed to raising $75 million for combating malaria, a preventable and curable disease. The rallying cry has been to eliminate deaths from malaria during our lifetimes.

The WHO recognizes that approximately half the world's population, or 3.2 billion people, are at risk of malaria, which is transmitted by female mosquitos. The WHO reports that "between 2000 and 2015, malaria incidence [the rate of new cases] fell by 37 percent globally. In that same period, malaria death rates fell by 60 percent globally among all age groups, and by 65 percent among children under five."[14]

IMPROVING GLOBAL HEALTH, ONE SHIPPING CONTAINER AT A TIME

"Really, when I retired, I had a wonderful new career," said Colin Wilkinson, a former petroleum company executive who had planned to do some consulting in that industry in retirement. "I got so involved in missions that I didn't have time to work. So it made a beautiful transition for me."

Now living in College Station, Texas, and chairing Christ United Methodist Church's Global Outreach team, he continues a pursuit he started while living in Houston: transforming shipping containers into medical clinics.

"I've been going to Maua Methodist Hospital in Kenya for the last sixteen or eighteen years, taking mission teams," Wilkinson said. The hospital is far from any major city, so teams from the United States would help its staff set up "bush clinics" in small villages with no regular medical care available.

"You held a clinic under a local acacia tree, or in a school, or some kind of canopy that you had, and it was the best you could do," he said.

Wilkinson heard about container clinics when he was a member of Chapelwood UMC in Houston. He learned that these large metal shipping containers—cheap, sturdy, portable, and many of them the size of two or three rooms—can be deployed anywhere in the world with the clinic already assembled within the container.

Wilkinson helped build a container clinic destined for Belize. Lakewood UMC then built one that stayed in Houston, answering a local need. So far, Wilkinson has played some part in bringing clinics to eight different countries. Missionaries or nongovernmental organizations keep them staffed and equipped to provide care.

When he moved to College Station, Wilkinson approached Maua Methodist Hospital with the idea.

"We said, 'How would you like to have a clinic that you could place at a location and use as a remote center?' ... They said, 'Well, that sounds like a great idea, let's try it.'"

Christ UMC's clinic took six or seven months to complete—about twice the time expected—but while the team was frustrated by setbacks, God used the delays for good. Sitting in the church parking lot near a four-lane highway, the clinic-to-be garnered attention.

"I have to say that God was smiling, because he was using it as a point of visibility. People were seeing it, asking questions about it," Wilkinson says.

A church from the Dallas area, First UMC of Duncanville, saw Christ Church's work in progress and followed its example; they recently returned from seeing their clinic installed in Panama. Churches from other states have contacted Christ Church, as well.

Locally, leaders of BUILD, a student-driven service organization at nearby Texas A&M University (buildtamu.com), saw the container while searching for new projects to unify the student body. They're outfitting four clinics per year, and plan to finish a total of twelve.

"This time, one is going to Haiti, one to Honduras, one to Greece, and one to Kenya, which will be the second one of the program that I mentioned earlier, with Maua Methodist Hospital," Wilkinson said.

Wilkinson traveled to Kenya for the opening of the first Maua container clinic.

"I think the first day that we opened, there were a thousand people there," he said. "They were all there singing and dancing and praising God and singing in Swahili, 'It is a miracle. Thanks be to God.'"

Before INM, one person in the world died of malaria every thirty seconds; that has now decreased to one every sixty seconds—still not acceptable but a significant improvement. The United Methodist Church has helped to make that happen. As of this writing, the denomination has raised just over 90 percent of its $75 million goal. Those funds have been targeted toward four key areas: distribution of treated bed nets, communication of lifesaving information to at-risk people, health facilities for timely treatment, and education.

To date, 2.3 million nets have been distributed, and improvements have been made in access to diagnostic tests and medication, as well as in infrastructure including improved water drainage and sanitation access. Approximately 4.6 million people have received important information about the prevention and treatment of malaria via new radio stations and access to hand-crank or solar-powered radios. Three-hundred-plus clinics are operated by The United Methodist Church in Africa. INM helps provide the malaria diagnostic tests and treatments needed. The UMC has also trained more than 11,600 local health workers who in turn train their communities about malaria.[15]

The war is not over, especially in sub-Saharan Africa. The WHO reported, "In 2015, the region was home to 88 percent of malaria cases and 90 percent of malaria deaths."[16] We need to stay engaged. But though the war continues, battles are being won.

In 2013, the Ginghamsburg Leadership Board committed to raising $1 million over five years toward malaria efforts in South Sudan as part of our annual Christmas Miracle Offering. Each Advent since 2004, we have challenged our church family to have a simpler Christmas and to spend only half as much on their own family as they normally would while bringing an equal amount for the offering. The miracle offering has enabled us to invest more than $8 million since 2005 into sustainable humanitarian projects both locally and globally.

More than half of the pledged INM money has been raised and used to distribute thirty thousand treated nets in Yei County of South Sudan. Also, funds have provided for medication and treatment as well as for additional nets to protect some of the most vulnerable malaria victims, young children and pregnant mothers. It has been a privilege to be part of an investment where we can see visible results. It is also heartbreaking to travel to the communities our investment has supported and to hear the stories and see the faces of those who have suffered and struggled, often repeatedly, as well as the faces of those who have lost loved ones to malaria.

It is difficult to find someone in Yei who has not experienced a loss. The last time a Ginghamsburg mission team visited the site of our work in Yei, they met a woman named Solange. I have not been able to get her picture out of my mind. Solange, who has given birth to nine children, explained to our team that Africans have large families because they lose so many children to malaria and other preventable diseases. Sadly, Solange knows this first-hand. Tresor, a surviving son, has suffered and recovered from malaria multiple times and is a frequent visitor to one of the clinics we have helped support.

In 2014 the staff videographer and chief storyteller of our Ginghamsburg team, Dan Bracken, created a powerful documentary about UMC efforts against malaria in South Sudan. I encourage you to visit YouTube.com and search for "The Sudan Project: War on Malaria" to view it. It is well worth the twenty-three minutes of viewing time.

As Dan's video shows, we must allow our hearts to be broken by those things that break the heart of God.

HEALTH IN OUR OWN FRONT PEW

As critical as the church's focus is on killer disease and access to healthcare across the globe, we also can't afford to neglect our own backyard. We continue to experience significant health issues across the United States, and many are in a sense of our own making. In the chapter on leadership we talked about the need to mind the gap between what we believe and what we actually do. The unfortunate example was United Methodist clergy, who espouse a belief in taking care of God's temple and yet engage in behaviors that lead to obesity rates that are above even the rest of the American public.

Despite increasing awareness and focus, adult obesity continues to rise in the United States. The Centers for Disease Control (CDC) reported in November 2015 that the percentage of American adults who were obese was over 36 percent in 2011–2014.[17]

If we look at more detailed demographics, the study results were even more alarming. The report indicated, "The prevalence of obesity among non-Hispanic black women was 56.9% compared with 37.5% in non-Hispanic black men. The prevalence of obesity was 45.7% among Hispanic women compared with 39.0% in Hispanic men."[18] Not to be overly dramatic, but this is a crisis.

Obesity by itself is not the worst of it; it's the killer diseases caused by obesity. Here are the top ten causes of death in the United States in order of impact:

- Heart disease
- Cancer
- Chronic lower respiratory disease
- Accidents

- Stroke
- Alzheimer's disease
- Diabetes
- Influenza and pneumonia
- Kidney disease
- Suicide[19]

Obesity can be a key contributor to three of the top ten: heart disease, stroke, and diabetes. Heart disease is the biggest killer, causing 23.53 percent of all deaths in the United States or taking over 611,000 lives annually. Heart disease is costly not only in terms of life but also dollars. In the United States, coronary heart disease costs $108.9 billion each year.

The guaranteed death rate across the entire US population living today is 100 percent, unless Jesus returns soon. But we don't have to be in such a big hurry about it. Risk for heart disease is greatly reduced when we eat healthfully, exercise regularly, stop drinking excessively, quit smoking, and manage stress. Dying is inevitable; premature death by heart disease is preventable and often a personal choice.

Stroke, the fifth leading cause of death in the United States, is somewhat less predictable or controllable. At the same time, we can take proactive measures to reduce our risk, such as controlling high blood pressure and cholesterol through medication, weight management, and diet, as well as by not smoking.

Diabetes represents nearly 3 percent of all US deaths. Type 1 diabetes is unavoidable; type 2 diabetes is more preventable. Regular physical activity and maintaining a healthy body weight are crucial.

With this in mind, Ginghamsburg promotes two 5K events each year. One each April benefits our New Path Outreach ministry. A second "Turkey Trot" run on Thanksgiving morning supports both New Path and our Sudan Project. I love that these runs combine meaning and mission with advocating an active lifestyle. Often church attendees will cluster in small groups or pairs a few months before each event to start training.

When Ginghamsburg built the Avenue youth building, we converted one of the classrooms into a small fitness center that is open six days a week. Minimal membership fees of $50 annually for regular Ginghamsburg worship attendees or $150 for non-attendees do not fill our coffers by any means but do provide the means for maintaining and replacing equipment. At various times, servants have started group ministries for walking, running, or biking. We use our bulletin, social media, and website to promote those to the larger church family.

Although Ginghamsburg as a church does not offer a direct health clinic, through New Path and other outreach initiatives we promote various dental and medical service opportunities for those who otherwise struggle to pay for health care.

In Romans 12:1, the Apostle Paul urges us, "in view of God's mercy, to offer your bodies as a living sacrifice, holy and pleasing to God—this is your true and proper worship." Paul returns to the theme in 1 Corinthians 6:19-20: "Do you not know that your bodies are temples of the Holy Spirit, who is in you, whom you have received from God? You are not your own; you were bought at a price. Therefore honor God with your bodies."

Sometimes I believe sinning against our own bodies and passively allowing others to do so is one of our greatest continuing failures in the American church. Jesus came that we might have life and have it abundantly (John 10:10). Jesus cares about the entire person—spiritually, physically, emotionally, mentally, relationally. Shouldn't Jesus' church do so as well?

TEXTING TO SAVE LIVES
(CONGO)

In remote villages of Africa, medical help may be a day's travel away. It's not uncommon for villagers to make the long journey only to find that a doctor isn't there or that needed medication isn't in stock.

The Reverend Betty Kazadi Musau, a United Methodist clergywoman from the Democratic Republic of Congo and a public health care worker, was an early adopter of a telecommunications project to improve communication between clinics and villages through mobile phone and texting technology.

Musau received a grant to show how text messaging and mobile health technology could be utilized in the developing world. Partnering with Medic Mobile; United Methodist Communications; and The United Methodist Church of the Resurrection in Leawood, Kansas, Musau designed the project to connect clinics and villagers via mobile messaging for four purposes:

- disease surveillance, monitoring outbreaks across regions
- drug stock management, to make sure drugs are resupplied or redirected to meet needs
- staff allocation
- important antenatal care

Musau said that during a February 2014 cholera outbreak, unnecessary deaths were avoided through messages to affected areas via the free text-messaging system. She simply sent texts reminding people to boil their water before drinking and to wash their hands frequently.

Musau reports: "A woman told me (that) messages to the villages to wash their hands before breast-feeding and before handling food worked to save lives."

—Adapted from an article on UMCom.org
(Courtesy: United Methodist Communications)

SELF-LEADERSHIP

All leaders within the church, whether clergy or laity, need to talk the talk, walk the walk, and provide practical application for the people we disciple in terms of physical health. I did not always see that as part of my role as a pastor, until I had a significant wakeup call. As a pastor, homeowner, husband, and father of two, I was incredibly busy in my thirties and forties. Eating often meant a quick, cheesy plate of microwaved nachos after a late-evening arrival at home following yet another committee meeting. Exercise meant dashing between meetings (worst-case scenario) or coaching my son's Little League baseball team (best-case scenario). By the time I hit my early forties, my body fat was 34 percent. I still looked fairly trim, except for a burgeoning paunch around my middle, but of course thin does not in and of itself equate to healthy.

One evening when I was forty-nine, Carolyn and I were eating dinner out in Cincinnati with my sister and brother-in-law when I collapsed and found myself lying in Carolyn's lap. I was rushed to the hospital with an arrhythmic heartbeat and blood pressure that had dropped to 60/40. I recovered from the incident quickly but knew that something had to change—*I* had to change. I found a trainer in the congregation and dramatically transformed my diet and exercise strategies. I announced the changes to the congregation as a surefire way of creating thousands of accountability partners. I have never looked back.

In my book *Momentum for Life*, I write about the need for self-leadership, a prerequisite for leading others. To achieve self-leadership, I need DRIVE, an acronym for five core practices:

- Devotion to Christ
- Readiness for lifelong learning
- Investing in key relationships

- Visioning for the future
- Eating and exercising for life

All five practices are important, but if I don't achieve the final item, I may not live long enough to model the first four.

Remember what business guru Stephen Covey says: "You can't kill the goose that laid the golden egg."[20] Self-care is not selfish; it is essential if we want to keep producing golden eggs.

THE ADDICTION EPIDEMIC

Before we leave the topic of killer diseases, we need to note one disease that has reached epidemic proportions in many communities: heroin addiction. Addictions kill more than the body—in a sense, they also kill the soul. Just this past fall, the CBS news program *Sixty Minutes* did a special story on heroin addiction in Ohio, my home state and first place of mission. The story starts with this observation:

> You might think of heroin as primarily an inner-city problem. But dealers, connected to Mexican drug cartels, are making huge profits by expanding to new, lucrative markets: suburbs all across the country. It's basic economics. The dealers are going where the money is and they're cultivating a new set of consumers: high school students, college athletes, teachers and professionals.[21]

The reporter interviewed Ohio Attorney General Mike Dewine, who said of heroin, "There is no place in Ohio where you couldn't have it delivered to you in fifteen, twenty minutes."[22] The National Institute on Drug Abuse reported a five-fold increase in deaths from heroin overdose between 2001 to 2013.[23] I suspect that none of our communities remains unscathed.

Recovery ministry was an early focus during my tenure at Ginghamsburg, when we opened up our sanctuary for Alcoholics Anonymous meetings. Now Ginghamsburg's Next Step Recovery worship on Saturday nights and the 12-Step groups it fosters and supports are an essential part of our "global health" focus.

A great example of these groups is Joshua Recovery Ministries (JRM). One of the 501(c)(3) organizations birthed by a Ginghamsburg member, JRM is supported annually by our Christmas Miracle Offering. JRM's housing program for men includes professional Christian counseling and a life coach to help each man develop and implement a life recovery plan. During the six-month program, each resident is also made part of daily devotions, required to attend 12-Step meetings, expected to be in a recovery-based church worship weekly (often Next Step), and encouraged to participate in mission work. One of JRM's houses is literally across the street from the back door of our Fort McKinley campus, and some residents frequently attend church or serve at the Fort.

Addiction of all types represents one of the most destructive health issues in our church neighborhoods and local mission fields. Addiction not only destroys individuals' lives but also those of whole families and even entire communities. One denomination-wide program that has been created in response is the United Methodist Special Program on Substance Abuse and Related Violence. SPSARV provides resources, guidance, and networking opportunities for proactively addressing the disease of addiction. Learn more at http://www.umspsarv.org.

Many churches support 12-Step programs or provide some type of recovery worship; however, much remains for us to do as Christ's advocates for healing in a suffering world.

MENTAL HEALTH: WE MUST DO BETTER

I was saddened to see suicide on the top ten list of killers in the United States. Suicide results in just over 1.5 percent of deaths each year, or 41,000 adults, but the death rate does not tell the entire story. Approximately 8.3 million adults report having suicidal thoughts over the course of a year. Among those aged fifteen to twenty-four years old, there are between one hundred and two hundred attempts for every completed suicide.[24]

Our Ginghamsburg Church family has lost two folks to suicide over the past eighteen months—one a teen and one a husband, father, and grandfather in his late fifties. That is by no means typical of our congregation, but it is of grave concern nonetheless. Traditionally these are not topics we have handled well in the church. Christian laypeople put on a "happy face" as we slide into our pews on Sunday morning. Lifeway Research reports that even though one in four Americans in any given year suffer from some kind of mental illness, two-thirds of Protestant senior pastors seldom speak about it.[25]

The news-garnering suicides of Robin Williams and the son of Saddleback Church pastor Rick Warren have brought visibility to depression, mental illness, and suicide. Following their son's suicide, Pastor Rick Warren and his wife Kay were interviewed on CNN, in what interviewer Piers Morgan described as his "most inspiring interview ever."[26] The interview aired just hours after Lifeway released research indicating that "Evangelical, funda-mentalist, or born-again Christians (48 percent) agree prayer can overcome mental illness. Only 27 percent of other Americans agree."[27] The church clearly has some catching up to do.

The stigma we place on mental illness must stop, and better education and intentionality must begin. As Kay Warren declared in the CNN interview, referencing 1 Corinthians 15:43, "Matthew's body was broken. That gun broke his body, and he was buried in brokenness. But he's going to be raised in glory."[28]

Ginghamsburg's nonprofit New Creation Counseling Center works hard in meaningful practical and spiritual ways to serve those who struggle emotionally, mentally, or relationally. Ongoing support groups such as GriefShare and DivorceCare are also part of our strategy. But we must continue to ask as a church and as individual Jesus-followers: What more needs to be done?

God is a God of whole-life health. Christ expects his church to engage actively in reaching the lost and setting the oppressed free—free from the physical, mental, emotional, and spiritual barriers that rob all God's children of abundant life.

- If you are a pastor or church leader, you cannot lead others where you yourself are unwilling to go. Implement and model healthier habits that reflect eating and exercise for abundant life.
- Reach out to the recovery community. If you are not ready or called to start a recovery worship service, how can you make your space available for local 12-Step groups or serve within recovery-focused treatment centers?
- Do you have open spaces available for activity and exercise in your facility during early morning, weekend, or evening hours? Offer fitness classes or start fitness ministries such as running or biking clubs.
- Host a community health fair. Involve doctors or other medical professionals from your church community in its planning and execution.
- Bring mental health issues into the light. Speak from the pulpit about mental health. Let people know where they can turn for professional and spiritual care. Welcome all to find healing, whether from physical, emotional, or mental health challenges.
- If your church is large enough to have a staff team, does the church have an employer-provided wellness program? In order for Ginghamsburg staff members to receive the full church-provided funding available toward their health insurance deductible, they must complete certain health assessments, medical exams,

or tests based on age and gender within each current insurance plan year. Prevention and early detection are keys to improving health.

- Commit to being part of Imagine No Malaria. (See imaginenomalaria.org.)
- Visit umcmission.org, and explore how you and your church can become part of United Methodist global health initiatives around the world. Research and support other global health efforts, such as those described at GBGM.org, the website of The United Methodist Church's General Board of Global Ministries.

Epilogue

O for a thousand tongues to sing, my great Redeemer's praise, the glories of my God and King, the triumphs of his grace!
  Charles Wesley, "O For a Thousand Tongues to Sing"

Christ's church at this still-early point in the twenty-first century is clearly not perfect. In 2015 the Pew Research Center reported that mainline denominations in particular are struggling. Within the past seven years, the percentage of all Americans who identify with a mainline denomination has decreased from 18.1 percent to 14.7 percent.[1] In the meantime, America's religiously unaffiliated increased 7 percent in the same seven-year window. The Towers Watson Report also told a somber and sobering tale.

However, Jesus does his best work in cemeteries, and we are not dead yet! Far from it. Christ's church may not be perfect, but we serve a Messiah who is. Our years ahead are poised for powerful ministry and mission. We have identified the four areas of focus that lead to vitality; we stand on a sound theology; we have named the viable strategies. Now we just need to do it.

Perhaps the only real barrier to becoming the Passionate Church that will change the world is our propensity to focus more on things that divide us than on the gospel that unites us. Non-Christians must shake their heads as we vehemently argue among ourselves on social media and in backroom meetings about red cups, border walls, political candidates, and contentious theological points. As John Wesley once pensively asked, "Though we cannot think alike, may we not love alike?" He promptly answered his own question: "Without all doubt, we may."[2]

It's time for Christ's church to stop the doubting and start the doing. When John the Baptist was downcast, discouraged, and imprisoned, he sent his disciples to ask Jesus, "Are you the one who is to come?" Jesus responded, "Go back and report to John what you have seen and heard: The blind receive sight, the lame walk, those who have leprosy are cleansed, the deaf hear, the dead are raised, and the good news is proclaimed to the poor" (Luke 7:22).

That's God's preferred future picture for Christ's church as we disciple and launch passionate and principled Christian leaders, minister with the poor, create new and renewed churches, and offer to the world the abundant health of living in Christ.

Lord Jesus, let it be so. Amen.

Notes

INTRODUCTION

1. W. Stephen Gunter, "Methodism and the Missionary Imagination," *Divinity Magazine*, Duke Divinity School, Spring 2014 Volume 13, Number 2, accessed January 18, 2016, https://divinity.duke.edu/sites/divinity.duke.edu/files/divinity-magazine/165167_1_web.pdf
2. Tony Campolo, audio sermon, includes "It's Friday but Sunday's Coming" 2013, http://tonycampolo.org/its-friday-but-sundays-coming/#.VorTMDaC0yE.
3. David de Wetter, Ilene Gochman, Rich Luss, and Rick Sherwood, "UMC Call to Action: Vital Congregations Research Project–Findings Report for Steering Team," Towers Watson, June 28, 2010, p 23, accessed January 21, 2016, http://s3.amazonaws.com/Website_Properties/news-media/documents/umc-call-to-action-vital-congregations-research-project.PDF

4. Michael Lipka, "5 Key Findings about Religiosity in the U.S.— and How It's Changing," November 3, 2015, http://www .pewresearch.org/fact-tank/2015/11/03/5-key-findings-about -religiosity-in-the-u-s-and-how-its-changing/.

5. R. Green, Cassell's Popular Shilling Library, vol. 7, *John Wesley* (London, Paris, & New York: Cassell, Petter, Galpin, & Co., n.d. ca. 1881), 28.

6. Robert M. Solomon, *Jesus Our Jubilee: Finding True Liberation, Perfect Justice, and Everlasting Peace* (Singapore: Discovery House, 2015), e-Book.

7. See the chapter "Multiplication vs. Expansion" in my book *Change the World* (Nashville: Abingdon, 2010).

8. Howard Snyder, *The Community of the King*, rev. ed. (Downers Grove, IL: IVP Academic, 2004), 123.

9. "Primitive Physick: John Wesley on Diet and Excercise, [sic]" Faith & Leadership, July 30, 2012, https://www.faithandleadership .com/primitive-physick-john-wesley-diet-and-excercise.

10. "Overweight & Obesity Statistics," *National Institutes of Health, NIH Publication* No. 04—4158, updated October 2012, http:// www.niddk.nih.gov/health-information/health-statistics/Pages /overweight-obesity-statistics.aspx.

11. Howard Snyder, *The Radical Wesley and Patterns for Church Renewal* (Eugene, OR: Wipf and Stock, 1996), 116.

CHAPTER 1

1. For more information, see *Dare to Dream Pastor Program Guide* (Nashville: Abingdon Press, 2014). Available at http://images .umph.org/cokesburyportals/DareToDreamPPG_Final.pdf.

2. Clergy Health Survey Report 2015 (Glenview, IL: General Board of Pension & Health Benefits), accessed January 26, 2016, http://www.gbophb.org/assets/1/7/4785.pdf.

3. David de Wetter, Ilene Gochman, Rich Luss, and Rick Sherwood, "UMC Call to Action: Vital Congregations Research Project– Findings Report for Steering Team," Towers Watson, June 28, 2010, p 35, accessed January 21, 2016, http://s3.amazonaws.com /Website_Properties/news-media/documents/umc-call-to -action-vital-congregations-research-project.PDF.

4. John Wesley, "Scriptural Christianity," Sermon #4, http://www
.umcmission.org/Find-Resources/John-Wesley-Sermons/Sermon
-4-Scriptural-Christianity.
5. Andy Stanley, *Deep and Wide: Creating Churches Unchurched
People Love to Attend* (Grand Rapids, MI: Zondervan, 2012), 134.
6. Walter A. Elwell, ed., *Evangelical Dictionary of Theology*, 2nd ed.
(Grand Rapids, MI: Baker Academic, 2001), 1267.

CHAPTER 2

1. The World Bank, "Overview," updated October 7, 2015, www.
worldbank.org/en/topic/poverty/overview.
2. "Income and Poverty in the United States: 2014", https://www
.census.gov/content/dam/Census/library/publications/2015/demo
/p60-252.pdf.
3. Thomas Gnau, "Tony Hall to Lead New Fight against Hunger in
Dayton," *Dayton Daily News*, September, 10, 2015.
4. W. Huitt, "Maslow's Hierarchy of Needs," Educational Psychology
Interactive (Valdosta, GA: Valdosta State University), http://
www.edpsycinteractive.org/topics/conation/maslow.html.
5. Jack Palmer, "Hole-y Bible Gets a Digital Makeover," *Sojourners*,
November 1, 2011, https://sojo.net/articles/hole-y-bible-gets
-digital-makeover.
6. Philip Yancey, *The Jesus I Never Knew* (Grand Rapids, MI:
Zondervan, 1995), 115.
7. John R. Tyson, *The Way of the Wesleys* (Grand Rapids, MI:
William B. Eerdmans, 2014), 160.
8. Charles Edward White, "What Wesley Practiced and Preached
about Money," *Leadership Journal*, Winter 1987, http://www
.christianitytoday.com/le/1987/winter/87l1027.html?paging=off.
9. Skevington Wood, *John Wesley: The Burning Heart* (Grand Rapids,
MI: William B. Eerdmans, 1967), 142–44.
10. Tyson, *The Way of the Wesleys*, 171.
11. John Wesley, "The Use of Money," Sermon #50, accessed January
27, 2016, http://www.umcmission.org/Find-Resources/John-Wesley
-Sermons/Sermon-50-The-Use-of-Money.
12. Tyson, *The Way of the Wesleys*, 172
13. Ibid., 173.
14. Jeremy Taylor, *The Rules and Exercises for Holy Living & Dying*
(London: Bell & Daldy, 1857), 2.

Chapter 3

1. Skevington Wood, *John Wesley: The Burning Heart* (Grand Rapids, MI: William B. Eerdmans, 1967), 92.
2. Ibid., 94.
3. Ibid., 115.
4. Alan Hirsch, *The Forgotten Ways* (Grand Rapids, MI: Brazos Press, 2006), 20.
5. Ibid., 18.
6. Ibid., 19.
7. You can learn more about Embrace in Rosario Picardo's *Ministry Makeover: Recovering a Theology for Bi-vocational Service in the Church* (Eugene, OR: Wipf & Stock, 2015).
8. "Huber Heights development plans being revealed," *WHIO*, October 2015, 2015, http://www.whio.com/news/news /huber-heights-development-plans-being-revealed/nn6gt/.
9. "About," *Christian Community Development Association*, accessed January 28, 2016, http://www.ccda.org/about.
10. "Relocation," *Christian Community Development Association*, accessed January 28, 2016, http://www.ccda.org/about/ccd -philosophy/relocation.
11. "Reconciliation," *Christian Community Development Association*, accessed January 28, 2016, http://www.ccda.org/about/ccd -philosophy/reconciliation.
12. "Redistribution," *Christian Community Development Association*, accessed January 28, 2016, http://www.ccda.org/about/ccd -philosophy/redistribution.
13. "Planting," *Discipleship Ministries of The United Methodist Church*, accessed January 28, 2016, http://www.umcdiscipleship.org /new-church-starts.
14. "Vietnam," *Open Doors USA*, accessed January 29, 2016, https:// www.opendoorsusa.org/christian-persecution/world-watch-list /vietnam/.
15. Tom Gillem, "Mission Initiatives Birth New Faith Communities," *Interpreter*, January/February 2015, http://www.interpretermagazine å.org/topics/mission-initiatives-birth-new-faith-communities.

CHAPTER 4

1. Hebrew Dictionary (Lexicon-Concordance), accessed February 2, 2016, http://lexiconcordance.com/hebrew/3671.html.
2. John Wesley, M.A., *"Primitive Physick, or An Easy and Natural Method of Curing Most Diseases"* (London, June 11, 1747), accessed February 2, 2016, http://www.umcmission.org/Find-Resources/John -Wesley-Sermons/The-Wesleys-and-Their-Times/Primitive-Physick.
3. Julie Corliss, "Too Much Sitting Linked to Heart Disease, Diabetes, Premature Death," *Harvard Health Publications*, January 22, 2015, http://www.health.harvard.edu/blog/much-sitting-linked-heart -disease-diabetes-premature-death-201501227618.
4. *"Primitive Physick: John Wesley on Diet and Excercise,"* *Faith & Leadership*, July 30, 2012, https://www.faithandleadership .com/primitive-physick-john-wesley-diet-and-excercise.
5. "The Letters of John Wesley," Wesley Center Online, http:// wesley.nnu.edu/john-wesley/the-letters-of-john-wesley/wesleys -letters-1778/.
6. "Randy Maddox: John Wesley says 'Take Care of Yourself,'" *Faith & Leadership*, July 30, 2012, https://www.faithandleadership.com /randy-maddox-john-wesley-says-take-care-yourself,
7. "10 Facts on the State of Global Health," World Health Organization, June 2014, http://www.who.int/features/factfiles /global_burden/facts/en/.
8. Debra Goldschmidt, "Smoking Rate Continues to Decline Among US Adults," CNN, November 19, 2015, http://www.cnn.com/2015 /11/17/health/smoking-rate-decline/.
9. "10 Facts on the State of Global Health," World Health Organization, June 2014, http://www.who.int/features/factfiles /global_burden/facts/en/
10. "The Battle Against AIDS: AIM for Victory," *The Economist*, July 28, 2012, http://www.economist.com/node/21559620.
11. Maggie Fox, "'Extraordinary Progress' Against AIDS, 8 Million Lives Saved: Report," *NBC News*, July 14, 2015, http://www .nbcnews.com/health/health-news/extraordinary-progress-against -aids-report-n391861.
12. "UNAIDS congratulates newly elected Pope Francis," press release, March 14, 2013, http://www.unaids.org/en/resources /presscentre/pressreleaseandstatementarchive/2013/march /20130314pspopefrancis/.

13. United Methodist Global AIDS Fund, http://www.umcmission
    .org/Give-to-Mission/Search-for-Projects/Projects/982345.
14. World Health Organization, Malaria Facts Sheet, October 2015,
    http://www.who.int/mediacentre/factsheets/fs094/en/.
15. "How we are beating malaria," Imagine NO Malaria, accessed
    February 8, 2016, http://imaginenomalaria.org.
16. World Health Organization, Malaria Facts Sheet, October 2015.
17. "Prevalence of Obesity Among Adults and Youth: United States,
    2011–2014," NCHS Data Brief, No. 219, November 2015, http://
    www.cdc.gov/nchs/data/databriefs/db219.htm/.
18. Ibid.
19. Hannah Nichols, "The Top 10 Leading Causes of Death in the
    US," September 21, 2015, http://www.medicalnewstoday.com
    /articles/282929.php.
20. Stephen R. Covey, *The 7 Habits of Highly Effective People* (New
    York: Simon & Schuster, New York, 1989), 62.
21. Bill Whitaker, "Heroin in the Heartland," *60 Minutes*, November
    1, 2015, http://www.cbsnews.com/news/heroin-in-the-heartland
    -60-minutes/.
22. Ibid.
23. "Overdose Death Rates" National Institute on Drug Abuse,
    rev. December 2015, http://www.drugabuse.gov/related-topics
    /trends-statistics/overdose-death-rates.
24. Nichols, "The Top 10 Leading Causes of Death in the US."
25. Bob Smietana, "Mental Illness Remains Taboo Topic for Many
    Pastors," Lifeway Research, September 22, 2014, http://www
    .lifewayresearch.com/2014/09/22/mental-illness-remains-taboo
    -topic-for-many-pastors/.
26. Kate Shellnut, "Rick Warren Tells Story of Son's Suicide on
    CNN," *Christianity Today*, September 18, 2013, http://www
    .christianitytoday.com/gleanings/2013/september/rick-warren-tells
    -story-son-matthew-suicide-cnn.html.
27. Bob Smietana, "Half of Evangelicals Believe Prayer Can Heal
    Mental Illness," Lifeway Newsroom, September 17, 2013, http://
    blog.lifeway.com/newsroom/2013/09/17/half-of-evangelicals
    -believe-prayer-can-heal-mental-illness/.
28. Shellnut, "Rick Warren Tells Story of Son's Suicide," http://www
    .christianitytoday.com/gleanings/2013/september/rick-warren-tells
    -story-son-matthew-suicide-cnn.html.

EPILOGUE

1. "Christians Decline as Share of U.S. Population; Other Faiths and the Unaffiliated Are Growing," Pew Research Center, May 7, 2015, http://www.pewforum.org/2015/05/12/americas-changing -religious-landscape/pr_15-05-12_rls-00/.
2. John Wesley, "Catholic Spirit," Sermon #39, http://www .umcmission.org/Find-Resources/John-Wesley-Sermons/Sermon -39-Catholic-Spirit.

Facilitator's Guide
Jacob Armstrong

Introduction

When I read Mike Slaughter's manuscript for *The Passionate Church*, I was inspired. As a local church pastor, I was moved by his fire and conviction, and I felt a fire and conviction grow in me.

The call to raise up new leaders made me think how self-focused I have been and how I have ignored potential leaders in my church. The reminder of Christ's good news to the poor inspired me to look at my own life and ministry in light of how I am serving those around me. The chapter on starting new and renewed congregations caused me to question why our congregation hasn't started anything lately. The staggering global and local health data made me pause and remember how Jesus came and healed people not only spiritually but also physically.

When I read *The Passionate Church*, I was inspired. Then I set the book down and went to lunch.

How many books, I wonder, have I read that inspired me but did not move me to action? How many times have I felt convicted by the Holy Spirit, only to move on quickly to the busyness of life and in so doing ignore the Holy Spirit?

I assure you, the purpose of *The Passionate Church* is not just to inspire you, make you think, lead you to have conversations, and then go to lunch. The hope for this book is that you will be moved by the same fire and conviction that filled the early church disciples and the pioneers of the Methodist movement and that this inspiration will cause you to act. The hope is that you will gather with those who aren't ready to give up on the church and do the hard work of considering what the next steps might be for you and your congregation.

This Facilitator's Guide is intended to help you with that follow-up. It is designed to help small groups of pastors and church leaders—perhaps eight to ten people in one church or across several churches—gather together, review the ideas about the Four Areas of Focus, and then move step by step through a process of putting those ideas into action in your church and community. Make a commitment to meet four times, one meeting for each of the four book chapters.

Each week begins with **Getting Started.** This section primes the pump for the conversation to follow and, through prayer, sets the stage for the gathering. The assumption is that everyone in the group has come prepared to share around the assigned chapter for that week.

Where Are We Now? allows an honest assessment of the current reality. There is no need for sugarcoating in this section. Questions are provided that allow for a deeper dive into the subject matter and how it relates to your present situation.

Where Do We Need to Go? asks each group member to consider carefully and prayerfully: What is a good first step that my church could take to improve in this area (a) this week, (b) this month, (c) this year?

How Can We Help Each Other? asks the group to offer support and encouragement to each other in taking the next action steps. This section will allow for mutual accountability in each of the four areas. At the conclusion of each session is a final thought or thoughts that will allow for further conversation if time permits.

The group time described in these pages has the potential for you and your church to take important steps toward life and vitality. As Mike Slaughter says, let's get started!

1

Developing Principled Christian Leaders

GETTING STARTED

In the Introduction, Mike Slaughter presents data that is often used to indicate the impending and even imminent death of the mainline church. For many of us who serve and lead in the church, this research makes our hearts ache as we see its reality on a daily basis. And yet our hearts come alive when we begin to affirm together that it is Friday, but Sunday's coming!

Before we jump into the first area of focus, spend a few moments as a group talking about our perceptions of the church's current reality and our hopes for its future.

- How do we feel when faced with the stark data marking the decline of the church not only numerically but also in mission and ministry?
- What leads us to read this book, engage in this conversation, and still hold out hope for the church?
- As we consider our current ministry context, in what ways can we proclaim "It's Friday, but Sunday's coming!" to those who may be close to giving up?

We wouldn't be reading this book and participating in this group if we weren't deeply committed to the beauty of the church and its certain glorious future. All of us still hear the whispers of our first call to be a part of this messy, beautiful church, and we are not ready to give up hope. Let's pray together as we begin to go deeper in the first vital area.

God, we know that the church is dependent on your Holy Spirit's power, not our own. And yet you invite us to participate, serve, and even lead in it. As we acknowledge that you never give up on us, we commit ourselves again to you and our calling within the Body of Christ. Open our hearts to the same spirit that gave birth to and empowered your people long ago. Amen.

WHERE ARE WE NOW?

Mike writes, "Clearly, equipping the saints by empowering the priesthood of all believers is essential for accomplishing the mission of Jesus." The early church movement and the early Methodist movement were clearly tied to the ability of the community of faith to develop principled Christian leaders. Thriving movements, such as the one we need today, always start with transformed leaders giving attention to growing more transformed leaders. With the scope of all that needs to be done, it is tempting for the called and empowered church leaders to seek to do everything themselves. This temptation is as old as the calling. Instead, what is needed is more attention given to developing other leaders. This is difficult because it means we must stop doing some of the work that is so important to us and start entrusting it to others.

Consider:

- How is my church doing in the area of Developing Principled Christian Leaders?
- What are we doing well? What are we doing poorly?
- How are leaders currently developed? Is there any intentional process for this?

WHERE DO WE NEED TO GO?

What is a good first step that my church could take to improve in this area (a) this week, (b) this month, (c) this year? Some questions to consider:

- How could the process of identifying leaders look different for us? (Consider Paul's list in 1 Timothy 3, Samuel's selection of David, and Mike's use of the three W's—wisdom, work, and wealth.)
- Keeping in mind that there is no cookie cutter for making church leaders, what does a "principled" Christian leader look like in our context? What is our end goal?
- What do I need to stop doing? What needs to be entrusted to someone else?

HOW CAN WE HELP EACH OTHER?

We have acknowledged that raising up new and principled leaders is essential for the task of church revitalization. But it's not a solo sport, and we are doomed to burn out if we take it on alone. In Jethro, Moses had someone who came alongside him, saw things he couldn't see, and gave counsel that was life-giving and perhaps even lifesaving. Each week we will consider how we can mutually support each other and how we can hold each other accountable to that which we ask to be held accountable.

- What did we hear in this time that gave us new perspective on our ministry situation or setting?
- What one or two things does each of us want to do this week that we can ask each other about next week? (Perhaps this could be the first step we named above.)
- How can we stay connected this week for mutual support and encouragement?

FINAL THOUGHT

We know that we cannot develop principled Christian leaders if we ourselves are not growing as principled Christian leaders. What intentional ways are you growing as a leader so that you can help others grow?

2
Engaging in Ministry with the Poor

Begin by having each person share how things went with the one or two steps they had planned to do this past week in the area of Developing Principled Christian Leaders. What went well? What didn't? What still needs to be done in this important area?

GETTING STARTED

As a twenty-seven-year-old pastor, I was invited to be part of a one-year mentoring program with Mike Slaughter. Thankfully, after the year ended Mike continued to make time for me. We have shared many phone calls, late-night conversations, and early-morning cups of coffee.

From those times, I can tell you that Mike has one "broken record" message that you will hear again and again. The first time I heard it was when I met Mike; he was standing in the old, original Ginghamsburg Church sanctuary that is now used for a variety of ministries of the church. The last time I heard it was the last time I talked to him. The message: *If it isn't good news to the poor, it isn't good news!*

In Luke 4, a passage known as Jesus Announces His Ministry, Jesus turns to a Scripture from Isaiah where we hear clearly the gospel priority, what Mike refers to as Jesus' mission statement:

- Good news to the poor
- Healing of the brokenhearted
- Liberty for captives
- Sight to the blind

When Jesus proclaims his priority, it naturally follows that this becomes the priority for the church, a message we must remind each other of again and again.

As our group begins its time together, let's allow some time for all members to describe a moment when they felt called into sharing Jesus' good news to the poor.

- What emotions did we feel?
- What were we led to do?

We have experienced the power of connecting with Jesus' mission for the world. Let us begin by offering together a prayer of openness to a deeper understanding of and commitment to Jesus' good news to the poor.

God, break our hearts for what breaks yours. Forgive us for the ways we have ignored the cry of your people and the call to serve. Open our minds and hearts now to consider how your church must be in ministry with the poor in our communities and our world. In Jesus' name. Amen.

WHERE ARE WE NOW?

Many of our churches are committed to ministries that serve those in need. Mike makes a distinction, though, between ministries for the poor and with the poor. Something different happens when ministry becomes cooperative, not a more privileged group giving and a less privileged group receiving. Another way of putting it is that we should move from being a church that has a missions budget for the poor to becoming a church that is on a mission with the poor–with the clear understanding that all of us are poor. Ministry with the poor is our second vital indicator of churches that are thriving, and it is a requirement for those of us who seek to stay connected to Christ's mission.

Mike talks about converting a consumer "serve us" mind-set to one focused on producing God's blessing within the lives of others. To put it mildly, this is a difficult task. The Luke 4 passage we looked at above, besides being called Jesus Announcing His Ministry, is also sometimes referred to as Jesus Rejected at Nazareth. When we begin the challenging work of turning an inward church into an outward church, we should be prepared for critique and even opposition. And we must understand that change does not happen overnight.

- What is the current state of my church as it relates to ministry with the poor?
- What are we doing well? What are we doing poorly?

Some questions to consider:

- Is there a scarcity mentality?
- Currently, where are we using most of our resources (people and finances)?
- Are people looking for permission to do risky ministry?

WHERE DO WE NEED TO GO?

What is a good first step that my church could take to move toward ministry with the poor (a) this week, (b) this month, (c) this year? Some questions to consider:

- What first conversations do we need to begin (or continue) in our church?
- Is there anything we will have to stop doing to begin this kind of work?
- Where will we face opposition?

How Can We Help Each Other?

Take a moment to consider the link between chapter 1, Developing Principled Christian Leaders, and chapter 2, Engaging in Ministry with the Poor.

- How can we develop and deploy people for the critical ministry needed with the poor?
- Can we identify people who need us to pour kerosene on their burning bushes?
- What did we hear in this time that gave us new perspective on our ministry situation or setting?
- What one or two things can each of us do this week that we can ask each other about next week? (Perhaps it could be the first step from the previous activity.)
- How do we need to stay connected this week for support and encouragement?

Final Thought

When John Wesley engaged in his risk-taking mission with the poor, it did not always fit the existing structures and norms of the established church. What potential barriers do you see in the structure or norms of church that you will have to break down?

3

Creating New and Renewed Congregations

Begin by having each person share how things went with the one or two steps they had planned to do this past week in the area of Engaging in Ministry With the Poor. What went well? What didn't? What still needs to be done in this important area?

GETTING STARTED

In chapter 3, Mike tells about some of the people who were part of Ginghamsburg Church's early years. It is inspiring to hear the heritage of this now strong and vital church. Sometimes it's easy to forget that every church was once a new church. Each church we serve, whether seven or seventy years old, began as a dream on the heart of one or two individuals to reach new people for Christ. We may not know their names, but every church began with the investment of planters who sowed their prayers, their finances, and their lives to see something new grow.

- Do we know the story of how our church was started? If we do, share the story briefly and ponder together how that past might inform the future. What needs to be recaptured?
- When have we been part of starting something new in the church? Share how this experience was different from serving in established ministries.

Pray together this prayer to begin the time of sharing on the topic of Creating New and Renewed Congregations.

God, renew our hearts as we begin to dream about how you are calling us to multiply and expand our ministries to reach new people. We know that it is only by your Holy Spirit that our churches will be renewed and new ones will be birthed. Let us be the vessels through which your Spirit works for the renewal of your church. In Jesus' name. Amen.

WHERE ARE WE NOW?

While the church growth movement focused on expansion, the early church model for growth was multiplication. Rather than growing past a certain attendance barrier, the called-out people of God multiplied by starting new, smaller congregations. The future of church growth seems to include the creation of smaller, missional faith communities that look like the communities they are in.

We may not all feel called to church "planting," but we are all being asked to reach out to our communities in new and creative ways. Every church can and should create new ministries that reach new people.

In nature, healthy living organisms reproduce. In the same way, most successful new church starts or restarts come from healthy local churches. The church, ever striving to reach and serve more people, must meet people where they are and tailor each new community and new ministry to the people it seeks to serve.

- What is the current state of my church as it relates to creating new opportunities to reach new people?
- Are we open to new things? If not, what are the barriers?

Some questions to consider:

- Regardless of the church's size, how might our congregation be part of planting a new church?
- What natural opportunities for multiplication do we see? What opportunities for expansion?
- How have our past experiences prepared us for the new things to which God is calling us?

Where Do We Need To Go?

What is a good first step that my church could take to move toward creating a new congregation or renewing an existing one (a) this week, (b) this month, (c) this year? Some questions to consider:

- Who are the unreached people in our area? How can we learn more from and about them?
- Who needs to be a part of the conversations to start something new at our church?

How Can We Help Each Other?

Mike talks about three R's that can apply to church planting and renewal: relocation, reconciliation, and redistribution. Which one of these does each of us feel the most connection to as God calls us to start something new? Also consider these questions:

- What did we hear in this time that gave us new perspective on our ministry situation or setting?
- Are there ways in which the people in this group can partner together to be a part of starting a new church or renewing an existing one?
- What one or two things does each of us want to do this week that we can ask each other about next week? (Perhaps it will include the first step named previously.)
- How does this group need to stay connected this week for support and encouragement?

FINAL THOUGHT

Creating new spaces for new people will include leadership development and ministry with the poor. Discuss the intersections and interrelationships among these three vital areas that we have examined thus far.

4
Improving Global Health

Begin by having each person share how things went with the one or two steps they had planned to do this past week in the area of Creating New and Renewed Congregations. What went well? What didn't? What still needs to be done in this important area?

GETTING STARTED

I will never forget the first time I visited a community where there was no clean, safe drinking water. It was in rural Nicaragua. This one simple fact affected every facet of life for the people who lived there. Women spent the majority of their day traveling to a good water source to get water for cleaning, bathing, and drinking. For thirty years I had taken for granted that all I had to do was turn a faucet when I needed to brush my teeth, wash my hands, or get a drink.

Issues such as improving a village's drinking water may seem too big, too global, too much for us to take on. But the church has a role to play. Jesus gave us the mandate to heal the sick, so we must search for ways to improve the health of all people. The church I served, which was young and small at the time, began a partnership with a clean-water organization that has led to hundreds of people in Nicaragua having safe water wells in their communities.

- As we begin our time together, briefly share when we have seen the power of the local church as it aligned its resources to help with global or local health issues. How did that involvement affect our life and worldview?
- What role should the church play in the physical health of others?

In light of the staggering statistics presented in chapter 4 regarding global and local health, let us begin in prayer.

God, our hearts ache as we consider how many suffer around the world. As we consider our role in health and healing for all people, we turn our hearts to you. We know that you alone are the healer and restorer. Use us as part of your great work in the world. In Jesus' name. Amen.

WHERE ARE WE NOW?

Mike describes a number of areas in which the church holds responsibility for helping to heal others, such as world health issues, local health issues, and personal health issues including addiction and mental health. Certainly no church would be equipped to take on all these areas at one time. However, we cannot let the enormity of the challenge paralyze us and prevent us from taking action.

In our time together we will consider ways in which our churches can begin or continue to engage in the holistic health of the people in our communities and the world.

- What is my church's current level of engagement in global or local health ministries?
- What are we doing well? What are we doing poorly?

Some questions to consider:

- If we are not focused on the health and wholeness of all people, what are we focused on?
- As we identify what we are focused on, how could those ministries relate to ministries of healing?

WHERE DO WE NEED TO GO?

What is a good first step that my church could take to move toward more engaged ministries related to global and local health (a) this week, (b) this month, (c) this year? Some questions to consider:

- What present issues in our community could lead to natural opportunities for ministry?
- Keeping in mind that we can't tackle all the world's issues at once, what one or two places globally could our congregation have an impact?

HOW CAN WE HELP EACH OTHER?

As we seek to lead others to better health, we are reminded that we must not only talk the talk but walk the walk. Each of us has areas in our own life and in the lives of our congregation where changes in personal habits would make us healthier and more effective. Take some time to discuss where we and our congregation are now and where we need to go, as it relates to personal health.

- What did we hear in this time that gave us new perspective on our ministry situation or setting?

- How can those of us in this room partner together to have a bigger impact on global health?
- What one or two things can we hold each other accountable for regarding our personal health and the health of our congregation?
- What are some ways in which this group could stay connected as we finish our scheduled time together?

FINAL THOUGHTS

The Four Areas of Focus offer important ways to keep the church connected to our mission of making disciples for Jesus Christ. Let's look at the four areas again:

- Developing Principled Christian Leaders
- Engaging in Ministry with the Poor
- Creating New and Renewed Congregations
- Improving Global Health

In which of the four areas is our church currently doing well? Which one has the best opportunities for growth? What will we take away from this book and the time this group has spent together? What are we going to do differently?